The Palestinian Movement
in Politics

The Palestinian Movement in Politics

Paul A. Jureidini
William E. Hazen

Lexington Books
D.C. Heath and Company
Lexington, Massachusetts
Toronto

Library of Congress Cataloging in Publication Data

Jureidini, Paul A
    The Palestinian movement in politics.
    Bibliography: p.
    Includes index.
    1. Fedayeen. 2. Jewish-Arab relations—1967-1973. I. Hazen,
William Edward, 1933- joint author. II. Title.
DS119.7.J89   322.4'2'095694   76-17506
ISBN 0-669-00858-3

Copyright © 1976 by D.C. Heath and Company

Second printing August 1978

Published simultaneously in Canada

International Standard Book Number: 0-669-00858-3

Library of Congress Catalog Card Number: 76-17506

Contents

Preface

The Palestinians have been making headlines for several years. Primarily, these news items have focused on terrorist attacks, guerrilla raids into Israel, fighting in Lebanon and Jordan, or argumentations at the United Nations. As a result, many theories have arisen about them. This book attempts to explain the raison d'etre for the Palestinian guerrilla movement. The authors have traced the Palestinian movement from its origins in the 1920s to just prior to the Lebanese crisis of 1975. Specific topics discussed are the relations of the Palestinian revolutionary movement with the Arab states, the use of terrorism to attract worldwide attention and support among its people, and an assessment of its future in a Palestinian state. It is hoped the reader will find sufficient material to understand the Palestinians better.

Thanks must be extended to Dr. Peter Gubser in his compilation on terrorist events. Furthermore, it must be recognized that parts of this book were based on work performed for the Department of Defense.

The Palestinian Movement
in Politics

1 Introduction

The dilemma facing world leaders who are seeking a lasting peace in the Middle East was created in May 1948, when British forces withdrew from the mandated land of Palestine, thereby permitting the Jewish settlers immediately thereafter to proclaim the independence of a Jewish state. The subsequent defeats of the disorganized Arab armies, bent on the destruction of this fledgling state, which they claimed was illegal, established solidified Jewish control over an ever-expanding territory.

The origins of the dilemma may be traced to the latter part of the nineteenth century when Theodore Herzl, who favored the establishment of a national home for the Jewish diaspora, spoke to the Zionist congresses. The homeland idea gained credence with the inclusion in the Balfour Declaration of 1917 between France and Great Britain of a clause that called for the establishment of a Jewish home in Palestine. With Great Britain assuming the mandate for Palestine following World War I, the Balfour provisions were acceded to and Jewish immigration to Palestine grew in volume.

The Arab community, which formed the majority of the population living in Palestine, objected to and actively opposed the increase of Jewish immigration and any proposal designed to partition the mandated territory between the two communities. The organizational development of this Palestinian opposition can be divided into three phases: The resistance, or preorganization phase, which began in the early 1920s and ended in 1948 with the establishment of the state of Israel; the intermediate phase, beginning in 1949 and ending with the June 1967 war; and the insurgent phase, which began after the 1967 June war. (See figure 1-1.)

The Resistance Phase

The earliest reaction of the Arab Palestinian inhabitants to the implementation of the Balfour Declaration was the creation of the Muslim-Christian Committee. Composed mainly of notables from the Christian and Muslim communities, the committee decided, in July 1921, to send a delegation to London to present the Arab point of view. They failed to make an impression because "none of them had had any contact with the West, or spoke a word of any language other than Arabic and Turkish," and because

1

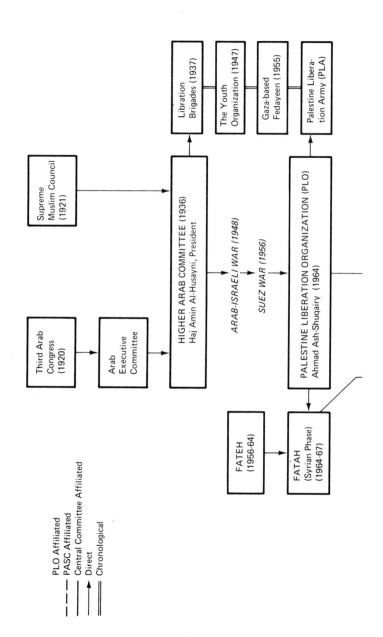

3

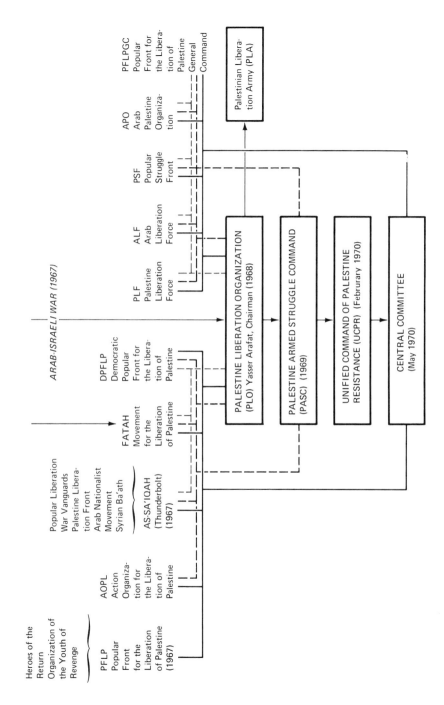

Figure 1-1. Genesis of the Palestinian Revolution, 1920-May 1970.

"they had no friends to advise them and no idea how to deal with the Colonial Office."[1] In essence the formation of this committee of notables was representative of the traditional approach used by a traditional society in its attempt to seek redress.

At about the same time the Third Arab Congress,[a] representing the leaders of the Arab Palestinian community, met in Haifa and established the Arab Executive Committee as a coordinating body. Gradually, the notables of the Muslim-Christian Committee united with the Arab Executive Committee.

The British, on the other hand, created in 1921 the Supreme Muslim Council and appointed Haj Muhammad Amin al-Husayni as its president. He was also elected Grand Mufti of Jerusalem. Although the Supreme Muslim Council was established as an autonomous body to regulate religious affairs of the Mandate—administration of the Waqf (religious property) and the Shari'a (religious courts)—Haj Amin al-Husayni quickly turned it into a council that presented as well the political interests of the Palestinian Arabs.[2] Able, talented, and unwilling to compromise or cooperate with the Mandate authorities, he was, as a result of special circumstances, to emerge as the only Arab Palestinian leader of stature.[3]

In the early 1930s a number of political movements were founded by the Palestinian notables. These movements—the Palestine Arab party (Jamal Husaini), the National Defense party (Ragheb Nashashibi), the Reform party (Dr. Husain Khalidi), the National Bloc (Abdul Latif Salah), the Congress Executive of Nationalist Youth (Yacoub Ghusein), and the Istiqlal or Independence party (Auni Abdul Hadi)[b]—were actually based on the extended family system, and were, at best, of the cadre type with no mass following.

The Arab Executive Committee, the Muslim Supreme Council, and the political movements of the early 1930s were similar in a number of aspects: They were urban centered, with no mass following, but able to incite urban mob violence; they were founded by the notables, almost all of whom were urban, and their membership was almost entirely composed of the landowning or mercantile urban classes; and they tended to

---

[a] In the days preceding and coming after the establishment of the British Mandate, Arab congresses were called to decide the political issues of the hour. The first two dissolved without accomplishing much, but the setting up of the Arab Executive Committee represents an effort to maintain continuity. The Fourth Arab Congress met in Nablus in September 1922 and decided that the Arabs should boycott the elections, which would have set up the British-sponsored Legislative Council.

[b] Prior to his becoming the focus for the opposition, Arab leadership had been diluted. The most affluent sought British favor and, therefore, tried not to disrupt the status quo. During this period, many of the largest land owners were living in Lebanon and Syria and profited from the sale of their Palestine land holdings to Jewish immigrants. The peasantry listened to their employers and, for the most part, remained quiescent.

view Zionism and Jewish immigration as a political threat that "ought to be tackled politically, that is, peacefully and at the lowest possible cost."[4] Thus, they tended to favor boycotts and strikes as a tool and resorted to limited violence only when it served to reinforce their demands.

In the countryside, however, an ever-increasing number of dispossessed peasants were beginning to view Jewish immigration and the Jewish land-acquisition program as an economic threat and a matter of life and death. As far back as 1925, the Mandate authorities had passed a series of economic measures that, in effect, resulted in more and more land becoming available for Jewish settlement. The first of these measures was the implementation of Article 6 of the Mandate, which called for the "close settlement by Jews on the land, including State lands and waste lands not required for public purposes."[5] Since most of the village pastures had been reclassified earlier as state land, settlement by the Jews seriously affected the villagers. By the time the harmful effort of this aspect of the measure was recognized and reversed, "many thousands of acres had been alienated and many peasants ruined."[6]

Even more damaging to the Arab Palestinians was the application: (1) of urban property tax to "unused land within the municipal boundaries"; (2) tithing (*ushur*) "to unused land in the countryside, the rate of tax in each case being assessed on a fictitious figure, an estimate of the revenue the land was capable of producing"; and (3) the abolishment of the Ottoman Land Bank, which was created by Young Turks "to provide easy credit for cultivators."[c] The bank was not replaced, but the tithing rate of 12.5 percent was reduced to 10 percent—the 2.5 percent having been that part of the tax used to augment the bank's capital. This repercussion for the Arabs was as expected: many urban proprietors were unable to meet the taxes on unused lands and were forced to sell their lands, primarily to Jews who had money available for land transactions. In the rural areas, most peasants borrowed from the village money lenders in order to retain their lands. But because of the high interest rates, sometimes as high as 60 percent per annum, their lands were lost through foreclosure.

By 1935 the number of small Arab Palestinian land owners, who had previously owned 50 percent of Arab Palestinian land, now were in possession of only 30 percent of the land.[7] Moreover, the policy of the Jewish General Labour Organization, the Histadrut, of pressuring Jewish enterprises into hiring only Jewish labor,[8] exacerbated the plight of the landless and the dispossessed by making it impossible for them to work on the

---

[c] It was later discovered that, frequently, the money lender had been financed by the Keyen Keremeth, a Jewish land-purchasing organization, which entered into contract with the money lenders to receive the foreclosed land. (See: Geoffrey Furlonge, *Palestine Is My Country: The Story of Musa Alami* (London: John Murray, 1969), p. 91).

lands they had once owned, or on which they had been hired to work. Most of them moved to urban centers in search of employment, only to find employment even more elusive (1) because of their general lack of skills, and (2) because most of the industrial enterprises were Jewish owned. As a result, the urban centers burgeoned with shantytowns, and the frustration and discontent of the unemployed brought the problems of the countryside closer to the Arab Palestinian political leadership.

The advent of the Nazis to power in 1933 further stimulated Jewish immigration to Palestine. This, in turn, resulted in two major developments: in the urban centers, the Arab Palestinian political position crystallized around the more militant leaders who, in March 1933, adopted the principle of noncooperation; in the countryside, Arab national committees were created in almost every village, and were usually headed by the village chief or the rural *ulema* (Muslim religious leaders and the equivalent of the Christian clergy).

By the end of 1935, when it became known that Jewish immigration had reached the unprecedented number of 61,000 per year, full-scale violence broke out. Arab violence and British countermeasures ended all chances of moderation and cooperation. The Arab Executive Committee was replaced by the Supreme Arab Council. In April 1936, the Supreme Arab Council was superceded by the Higher Arab Committee, with Haj Amin al-Husayni as its president. Its members had belonged to the various political movements that had come into existence in the early 1930s and were also the notables of the Muslim-Christian Committee and the Arab Executive Committee.[9]

In the countryside, where violence had broken out in December 1935, the rural masses rallied at first to the local *ulema* and their chief, Izz al-Din al-Qassam. Most of these *ulema* came from the lower "clergy," and their followers were mainly illiterate peasants. The appeal of Qassam and his collaborators to the rural masses, therefore, "could not be made except in religious terms," and "the battlecry was to defend the land and religion against the infidel."[10] Shortly after the death of Qassam and most of his aides in the first encounter with the authorities, the rural masses transferred their allegiance to Haj Amin al-Husayni, the Grand Mufti of Jerusalem. Thus, the Higher Arab Committee saw the fusion of the urban political leaders with the rural masses, and came to represent the political and economic interests of the Palestinian Arabs.

The task of the Higher Arab Committee, between 1936 and 1939, was, therefore, concerned with the organization and use of violence in the countryside as a means of pressuring the Mandate authorities to accede to the objective of keeping Palestine an Arab country. This objective included demands for: (1) an end to Jewish immigration, (2) "prohibition of the transfer of land from Arabs to Jews," and (3) "the establishment of a national government responsible to a representative council."[11]

It is not clear yet whether a split command between politician and fighter was intended by the Higher Arab Committee, or whether it resulted from the dispersal and imprisonment of the political leadership of the Higher Arab Committee after it had been outlawed in 1937 for the suspected murder of a British district commissioner. The Mufti sought refuge in Lebanon, where he continued to direct the activities of the suppressed Higher Arab Committee. But the operational command of the insurgents was entrusted to a Syrian: Fawzi al-Qawuqji. The Arab politicians, in their eagerness to maintain their control, "seemed convinced that a solution could be found once violence was stopped or brought under control."[12] They were thus willing to heed the advice of the Arab rulers in 1939, and accept a truce with the mandatory authorities without extracting, a priori, an agreement that could have insured the fulfillment of their objective.[d]

The course of the insurgency also may have contributed to the Higher Arab Committee decision to accept the truce. Although successful in bringing large parts of Palestine under Arab control, it was hamstrung by its inability to gain greater momentum. The areas brought under insurgent control were predominantly Arab inhabited, and most of the insurgents refused to venture beyond the immediacy of their villages. Qawuqji was encountering difficulties in his efforts to reorganize the insurgents into "Liberation Brigades," which would operate in all parts of Palestine, and had to rely on volunteers from neighboring countries. Local allegiance overshadowed attempts at interregional unity.

Insurgent parochialism, therefore, inhibited development of a genuine revolutionary movement, and this may have reduced the influence of the operational leadership. They were, in any case, willing to leave policy decisions to the political leadership. The political leadership, on the other hand, fearing the consequences of spent momentum, may have accepted the truce to preserve what had already been achieved. The net effort, however, was that the Palestinians never mastered the political use of violence.

The World War II years interrupted thoroughly the efforts of the Palestinians, and the insurgency never regained its momentum. The Grand Mufti, who had fled to Berlin, was temporarily discredited. The remaining leaders of the Higher Arab Committee, still in exile, were unable to control the course of events in Palestine where policy differences and petty jealousies had fragmented the Arab Palestinians. In the summer of 1943, the former leaders of the Istiqlal party succeeded in restoring partial uni-

---

[d] In October, 1936, the political leadership had also agreed, without condition and at the request of some of the Arab governments, to call off the general strike. It was, ostensibly, to allow the insurgents to participate in the harvesting of the orange crop. The decision almost destroyed the momentum of the insurgency during a crucial period, and is a reflection of the attitude of the leadership, which sought to reduce the costs of political action to its lowest levels.

ty. The Istiqlal demanded adherence of the Mandate authorities to the British White Paper of 1939 (limited Jewish immigration, no partition, and an independent state of Palestine). The partial success and position of the Istiqlal aroused the jealousies of other parties and provoked the Husaynis into founding the Arab Palestine party as an attempt to retain Palestinian leadership. Ultimately, the Husaynis reasserted their control, only to find that the League of Arab States had bypassed them in deciding the future of Palestine.[13]

When violence reemerged at the end of World War II, the Palestinian Arabs found themselves in the curious position of onlookers. The fight, this time, was between the Zionists and the British who seemed determined to adhere to the White Paper. At the same time, the pledge by members of the Arab League to protect the rights of the Arab inhabitants of Palestine, should the British fail to do so, obviated the need on the part of the Arab Palestinian leadership to mobilize their forces.

Jewish support at this time came mainly from the United States. Using the "holocaust" as their primary theme, Jewish organizations appealed to the sentiments of people everywhere to recognize the fact that the Jews were a stateless people seeking a home. The issue was brought eventually to the United Nations where a partition plan for Palestine was drawn up.

When it became apparent that the Zionists were beginning to gain the upper hand, and that the intervention of the Arab states was being affected by inter-Arab rivalries and United Nations debates, it was too late to resume the struggle. The flight of the Arab Palestinian urban elites was already under way, and the Arab Palestinian leadership could not rally an already divided and panic-stricken population. The resistance groups—the Arab Liberation Army, the al-Futuwah, and the an-Najjadah—which were hastily created, were no match for the Zionist organizations. They were generally ill-equipped, badly trained, and disorganized. With the exception of the forces that operated in the Jerusalem area under Abdel Khader al-Husayni, most of them were directed from abroad. Even the "Youth Organization," a sort of united Arab front established through the influence of the Cairo-based Muslim Brotherhood, failed to coordinate the activities of the separate resistance groups.[14] Playing the role of a Pontius Pilate, the British government withdrew completely from the political arena, leaving the Jews and Arabs to determine for themselves who would take control of Palestine.

The Intermediate Phase

The Palestinian issue is transformed, during this phase, and assumes a broader Arab character. The basicity of the issue—Palestinian Arabs versus Zionism—is diffused and becomes the Arab-Israeli conflict. The Palestinian Arabs lose their freedom of action, and become actors instead of directors, while the Arab countries adopt the Palestinian issue as their own, without, however, assuming specific responsibility for it.

As far as the eventual course of the Palestinian revolution is concerned, this phase is important because of three major developments. These were: the creation by Egypt of the Gaza-based Fedayeen; the establishment of the Palestine Liberation Organization (PLO); and the emergence of young "radicals" among the Palestinians.

A vicious cycle of border raids by Palestinian Arabs and Israeli reprisals soon developed after the conclusion of the armistice agreements in 1949. The Palestinian raiders consisted of three types: The first type was made up of raiders whose motives were thievery, "stimulated by the destitution and pervasive bitterness of the refugee camps."[15] The second type was composed mainly of the inhabitants of the Jordanian border villages "who were separated from their lands by the Armistics line,"[16] and who would either move in to collect crops planted by the Jewish settlers on the Israeli border, or actually move their herds onto the pasturelands they still considered as theirs. The third type consisted mainly of the followers of Haj Amin al-Husayni, and their purpose was political. Most of the reported incidents occurred in the Hebron area, the region around the Qalqilya salient, and in the Gaza Strip area.

In 1955 the Egyptian authorities and, specifically, Egyptian Army Intelligence, began to organize commando groups. Recruited from among the Palestinian refugees of the Gaza Strip, the commandos were both a tactical weapon (to hit specific Israeli targets), and a source of intelligence. It is not as yet clear what prompted the creation of these commando units, but the timing coincides with a number of events in the area.

A reported difference of opinion between President Nasser and the Grand Mufti, who moved his headquarters subsequently to Beirut from Cairo, may have at first impelled the Egyptian authorities to organize the Palestinians into Egyptian Army-affiliated commando units as a means of curbing the influence of Haj Amin al-Husayni. Israel's role in what is now known as the Lavon Affair[e] may have, on the other hand, hardened the Egyptian position and led them to use the commandos as a means of retaliation. Finally, the impending Egyptian-Czech[f] arms deal, and fears of

---

[e] Towards the latter part of January 1955, two Egyptian Jews convicted of an attempt to blow up the United States Information Service Library in Cairo on behalf of Israel were hanged. Israel protested the hangings claiming that it had nothing to do with the case. In 1960-61 Pinhas Lavon, the minister of defense during the crisis that led to the hangings in Cairo, admitted without revealing the nature of the operation, Israel's involvement in the attempted bombings. The damage had been done. It undermined a noticeable rapprochement between Nasser and Israeli Premier Moshe Sharett, and led the Egyptians to believe that Israel wanted in fact to destroy the good relations that existed then between Egypt and the United States, and impede the negotiations between Egypt and England over the evacuation of British troops from Egypt (For an excellent account of the "Lavan Affair" see: Ernest Stock, *Israel On the Road to Sinai* (Ithaca, New York: Cornell University Press, 1967), pp. 119-23.)

[f] Miles Copeland claims that President Nasser warned the United States as early as January 1955 that Egypt would conclude an arms deal with the Soviet Union if the United States did

a preemptive attack by Israel, may have moved the Egyptians to use the commandos for their intelligence-gathering requirements. The use of the Fedayeen by Egypt, however, proved to be one of the major catalysts of the 1956 war.

Since the Fedayeen were acting under Egyptian orders, their activities cannot be considered as a Palestinian attempt to pursue their struggle with Israel. Rather, the importance of the Fedayeen is to be found in the fact that some Palestinian guerrilla leaders who emerged shortly after the June 1967 war came from the ranks of these commando units.

In the spring of 1959 Arab involvement in the Palestinian issue led the United Arab Republic (then composed of a union of Egypt and Syria) to suggest the recognition of a "Palestinian entity" that could play an independent role in the Arab struggle against Israel. Later that year, Iraq proposed the creation of a Palestine Republic with provisional headquarters in the Gaza Strip and the West Bank. At a meeting of the Arab League Council in February 1960, Jordan countered with a proposal that called for the establishment of a Palestinian organization with headquarters in Amman, Jordan. The Jordanian plan stipulated, furthermore, that King Hussein would appoint the chairman of the organization, and that the organization would recognize the suzerainty of the King. The United Arab Republic then submitted a modified plan that proposed a Palestinian organization be established in every Arab state, representing thus the Palestinian community in those states, and that these organizations be merged at the Arab League level into one body.[17] Inter-Arab rivalries forced the postponement of any decision regarding Palestine until January 1964.

Israel and the related Palestinian question were issues common to most of the Arab states. But agreement on a common approach had to, first and foremost, take into account the national interests and sensitivities of the member states of the Arab League. President Nasser emerged from the 1956 war as the undisputed leader of the Arab world and hero of the Arab masses. It was natural, therefore, for the Palestinians to turn to him for a solution to their problem, and to accept his leadership. Nasser, in turn, could not ignore their presence, or refuse to heed their plea for action. Although his suggestion for an Arab recognition of a Palestinian entity was matched by similar declarations of interest on the part of some of the other Arab states, it also aroused their suspicion. Iraq, which had vied with Egypt for the leadership of the Arab world ever since the creation of the Arab League, had, under the regimes of Nuri as-Said and Abdel Karim Qassim, lost ground to President Nasser. It had to respond to Nasser's Palestinian challenge, but in a manner that would reduce his influence with the Palestinian community. Jordan, on the other hand, having

not furnish the Egyptian Army with the arms it had asked for. (See: Miles Copeland, *The Game of Nations* (London: Weidenfeld and Nicolson, 1969), pp. 132-33.)

annexed the West Bank with its large Palestinian population, could ill-afford to neglect the Palestinian entity issue now that it had been officially proposed. It also had to take into account the possible ramifications of an independent Palestinian Republic and the subversive potential of an Egyptian-oriented Palestinian organization.

For the Palestinian, the discussions that surrounded the recognition of a Palestinian entity by the Arab states represented a positive though hesitant first step. It was now up to the educated segment of the Palestinian community, which was most affected by this turn of events, to make it an irreversible first step. The fact that a Palestinian organization came to exist at all is, to a large degree, a result of the efforts of Ahmad ash-Shuqairy.

Shuqairy did not belong to the pre-1948 Palestinian leadership, nor to the factions that abounded within the Palestinian leadership during the late 1950s and early 1960s. He had served as head of the Saudi Arabian delegation to the United Nations from 1958 until September 1963, when he was dismissed from his post for refusing to present to the United Nations a Saudi Arabian complaint against Egypt. He was immediately appointed by the political committee of the Arab League to represent the interests of the Palestinian refugees at the United Nations. Shuqairy was thus eminently qualified "to head the type of organization which the Arab states were inclined to establish—an organization set up in their own image with the function of a quasi-government, and possessing a parliament and its own army."[18]

In the months preceding the Arab Summit Conference, which convened on January 13, 1964, Shuqairy played an instrumental role in reconciling Arab differences over an Iraqi plan submitted to the political committee of the Arab League in September. The plan envisaged the election of a Palestinian national assembly by popular vote among the Palestinians, and the formation of a government that would operate in both the Gaza Strip and the Jordanian West Bank. On January 18, 1964, Shuqairy was charged by the Arab heads of state with the task of establishing a Palestinian organization.[19]

The Palestinian Liberation Organization, which came to represent the Palestinian community, consisted of the National Congress, the PLO Executive Committee, and the Palestine Liberation Army (PLA).

The National Congress was composed of 422 popularly elected delegates representing the Palestinian community.[g] In its first meeting, which was held in May 1964, in the Jordanian section of Jerusalem, it acted as a constituent assembly that officially created the PLO and the Executive

---

[g] There is some question as to how representative these delegates were. Haj Amin al-Husayni and his followers refused to participate, and a number of other factions likewise boycotted the elections.

Committee. Thereafter, it was to assume a parliamentary function, and would meet at the request of the Executive Committee to consider matters affecting the Palestinian Community referred to it by the Executive Committee. The decisions of the National Congress then became binding on the Executive Committee. The National Congress was furthermore empowered to dismiss the Executive Committee or alter its composition.

The Executive Committee, composed of ten members and a chairman, assumed the role of a cabinet. It was responsible to the National Congress, represented the Palestinian community in official Arab circles, and could enter into agreements with any of the Arab states. In his official capacity as chairman of the Executive Committee, Ahmad ash-Shuqairy was thus in a position to place the following three demands before the Arab heads of state: "(1) freedom for the PLO to function as a supra-national entity among the refugees in every state, (2) the right to levy taxes upon them, and (3) freedom to draft the refugees into a Palestine Liberation Army."[20]

Although the Arab heads of state recognized the PLO as the official spokesman of the Palestinian community, they refused to allow it to draft the refugees into the PLA. Instead, the PLA was to be composed of Palestinian recruits contributed by the member states of the Arab League. The heads of state further limited the PLA's freedom of action by placing it under the control of the newly created United Arab Command (UAC). It was to be trained and equipped by the UAC.

The fact that the Palestinians would not be given any degree of independence by the Arab States, and that the Palestinian leaders during the intermediate phase would not seek to challenge Arab control, was recognized as far back as 1956 by a small group of Palestinians, then considered to be radicals or militants. One of these men was Yasser Arafat who, with several friends, founded al-Fatah (Harakat al-Tahrir al-Filastiniya). From the start, Fatah became an international organization with cells in numerous countries.[21] Members were recruited even from the Palestinian student organizations in Europe, although the majority of its membership came from the refugee camps in Gaza, Lebanon, Jordan, and Syria. Kuwait became the principal funding center. Above all strong ties were formed with the nationalists of Algeria who were at this time fighting their own liberation war. Syria became the headquarters of Fatah until the Syrian government attempted to clamp down on its operations, at which time Jordan became its principal base of operations with Beirut, Lebanon, its political center.

Another prominent revolutionist who sought to overcome the lethargy of the Palestinian people and the Arab governments was George Habash who, with Nayif Hawatmeh, helped found the Arab Nationalist Movement (ANM) in 1950.[22] Basically, when created, the ANM attempted to

unify all Arabs who believed in the Palestinian cause. Its members, therefore, cooperated fully with the Arab governments. However, by 1964, disillusioned with Nasser's inability to liberate their homeland, to prevent
the headwaters of the Jordan River from being diverted by Israel, by the
overt actions taken by the Arab states to dominate the Palestinians and to
involve them in inter-Arab rivalries, the ANM and Fatah decided to strike
out on their own by staging guerrilla attacks inside Israel. They disagreed
with those who believed that time was on the side of the Arabs, and insisted that time was on the side of the Israelis instead.[23]

The Insurgent Phase

The actions of Fatah and the ANM were to proliferate and to result in the
creation of numerous Palestinian guerrilla organizations whose basic goal
for each was to be the liberation of their homeland by force of arms. The
defeat of the Arab armies by Israeli forces in June 1967 enabled these militant Palestinians to gain control of the Palestinian nationalist movement.
Heretofore, the majority of the Palestinian community had been lulled
into a false sense of hope that they should be dependent upon the Arab
governments for the liberation of their country from its "Zionist usurp-
ers." The rapid capitulation of the Arab armies enabled the militants to
succor the Palestinians, and to push forward the idea that only they (Palestinians) would be able to control their own destiny. Only by means of
overt acts undertaken by themselves would the Zionist government be defeated.

Discredited, too, with the Arab governments was the leadership of the
PLO. These spokesmen who had assumed the mantle of leadership from
the Mufti who, on his part, had lost much prestige through his collabora-
tion with the Nazi German government during World War II, were now
forced to step aside for the militants. Ash-Shuqairy was replaced by Yahya Hammudah who was himself replaced by Yasser Arafat. This occurred
after the battle for Karameh on March 21, 1968, when al-Fatah was cata-
pulted to the forefront of the Palestinian movement. From this time on the
PLO has been dominated by the guerrilla organizations represented on
the Executive Central Committee, whose members form the majority of
the delegates of the National Congress.

The battle of Karameh was to be one of the watersheds of the Palestinian movement. Upon learning that Israeli forces were to launch a full-
scale retaliatory raid against their bases, the guerrilla leaders opted to
stand and fight with the Jordanian army.[24] When 15,000 Israeli armored
troops, supported by Patton M-48 tanks, moved across the Jordan River
toward al-Karameh, they found that guerrilla defenses were well-pre-

pared. In coordination with Jordanian artillery, the tank columns were stopped. Hand-to-hand fighting raged within al-Karameh itself and, although much of the town was destroyed, the guerrillas claimed a victory. An excellent propaganda campaign instilled in the Arab masses the idea that the Israeli withdrawal was a rout, and that Israeli dead numbered over 200. Although the facts were distorted, the guerrillas were able to emerge from the battle with honor at having fought the enemy without being defeated.

The Palestinian guerrilla organizations rode the wave of popularity through most of 1968. Recruits, not only from the Palestinian camps and other Palestinian communities throughout the Arab world but also non-Palestinian Arabs, poured into the training camps. Funds became plentiful, and Arab governments, recognizing the popular support given to the guerrillas, provided material and facilities. In Lebanon and Jordon the guerrilla organizations assumed control of the refugee camps and, especially in Lebanon, made them habitable for the first time.

Popular adulation was to run rampant among the Arab masses for many years. However, the rapid growth in number and size of the guerrilla organizations began to alarm the leaders of those governments that harbored the Palestinian refugees. When the Palestinian movement began to interfere in domestic as well as foreign affairs within the host countries, the die was cast for a confrontation. The first one occurred in Jordan in early November 1968, when a series of small incidents involving the guerrilla organizations caused the Jordanian army to clamp down on some of the offenders. Although quickly resolved, the incident portended future clashes between the growing power of the guerrillas and host central governments.[h]

The ensuing years (1968 to the present) have proven to be hard years for the guerrilla movement. After the Jordan debacle, when the Palestinian forces were defeated by the Jordanian army, the initial act was to reconstitute the movement. Several thousand had been lost in the fighting with Jordanian forces. Many more had been captured and imprisoned. Guerrilla forces in Syria, primarily as-Sa'iqa, became pawns of the government, with their freedom of movement curtailed. Iraq, while a strong supporter of the guerrilla movement, had refused to come to the support of the beleagured guerrillas in Jordan, even though fighting had raged around the Iraqi contingents stationed in Jordan. President Nasser had acted as mediator during the September 1970 clash but had died shortly after an accord had been reached. His successor, Anwar al-Sadat, was treading cautiously within his capital in an attempt to gain a political base. The Lebanese government, unable to check the massive influx of Pales-

---

[h] For a full discussion of the relations between the Palestinian and the host countries, see chapter 3.

tinians into its territory, had bolstered its positions on the border but was, in reality, powerless to attempt a "solution" as Jordan had just imposed. Weak, because of its religious segmentation, the Lebanese authorities attempted to govern by means of the accords reached in 1969.

The guerrillas, realizing that their last bastion was Lebanon, regrouped in the Arkoub and the camps located in Lebanon and settled down to live by the accords reached with the Lebanese government. It was a time when Arafat reached his zenith of power, when the more radical organizations—Popular Front for the Liberation of Palestine (PFLP) and the Popular Democratic Front for the Liberation of Palestine (DPFLP)—were at their nadir in strength and prestige. The PFLP had triggered the September clash by hijacking four planes to the Jordanian desert and then destroying them, in direct opposition to the wishes of Arafat and the moderates in the Palestinian movement.

There was some talk at the time that the guerrilla organizations were going underground.[25] If this had occurred, the movement would have had dire repercussions for Lebanon since containment would then have been virtually impossible. But the closing of several offices, including Fatah's in Beirut, signaled two things: that the guerrilla presence in Lebanon was being diminished and that consolidation was taking place under the PLO banner. Since Fatah was in virtual control of the PLO, the removal of several of its offices was no loss. Fatah business was then carried out from PLO locations.

The PLO underwent some change during 1971 when a new Executive Committee was formed. Fifteen in number, the committee included representatives of the leading guerrilla groups—Fatah, PFLP, the Arab Liberation Front (ALF), as-Sa'iqa, DPFLP, Popular Struggle Front (PSF), as well as the commander of the Palestine Liberation Army (PLA), and the head of the Palestine National Fund.[26] The Central Committee of the old format was disbanded since the new Executive Committee now represented all the organizations that had held positions in the Central Committee.

By incorporating the PFLP into the PLO, Arafat scored a big success for his policy of having the guerrilla forces unified under a single command. Splintering only dissipated guerrilla effectiveness. Arafat realized that he risked his prestige by backing PFLP membership since most of the moderate groups were opposed to Habash's organization, not only for its Marxist leanings but also for its terrorist policy. Arafat also realized that the PFLP, as a member, could disrupt the PLO. However, by taking the PFLP under its wing so to speak, the PLO would be able to exert some pressure, and, therefore, could hope to channel its activities into more acceptable ways.

In September 1971, some attempt was made by the Saudi government to mediate the differences between the Palestinians and Jordanians.[27] However, each side held to its view: the Jordanians demanded full control over the guerrillas, and the guerrillas demanded freedom of action within Jordan. The two positions hardened with the assassination of the Jordanian Prime Minister Wasfi Tal in Cairo on November 28, 1971, by four members of the Black September Organization (BSO).

The BSO became the phoenix that rose from the ashes of the Jordan debacle. Swearing vengeance against the Jordanian regime, dissident members of Fatah banded together and struck out against Jordanian targets. Tal was their first success. Seventeen days later the Jordanian ambassador to London, Zayd Ar-Rifai was wounded during an assassination attempt. On December 16, it was the turn of the Jordanian Ambassador in Geneva. A package exploded at his office. He was not involved, but three persons were wounded. The generally favorable publicity in the Arab world for these attacks enabled the guerrilla movement to recoup much of its lost prestige. They were still a force with which to contend—beaten, but not defeated.

During 1972 the Palestinian guerrilla organizations were involved with three significant yet diverse topics: unity, Lebanon, and terrorism. The PLO had held a congress in April, whose main thrust was to bring the different factions together under a single command.[28] The 151-member National Council passed several resolutions, foremost among those being the decision to form a Higher Military Council. Each organization would be represented on the council, which would coordinate all military operations. Above all, military units of the organizations would be merged under the command of this council. The Palestinian parliament also passed a resolution to establish the Information and National Guidance Department, charged with being the official source for all information concerning the Palestinian movement. Under its control, a news agency (WAFA) was to function as publisher. Furthermore, the radio broadcasts, "Voice of Palestine," would now be under its supervision. In spite of the trappings of unity, the most important one concerning the union of all Palestinian organization was left in abeyance.

Throughout the year, Arafat and his supporters tried unsuccessfully to achieve unity. Even a section of his own organization Fatah "mutinied."[29] The dispute arose when Arafat sought to bring into line all factions of his group to support his policies. The leader of the faction that refused to go along with his "moderate" stance was Abu Yusif al-Kayid, who believed that Arafat was betraying the goals of the Palestinian revolution. Al-Kayid refused to support Arafat when the latter called for the cessation of guerrilla operations against Israel from Lebanon and the withdrawal of guerrilla units from the more populous regions in southern

Lebanon.[30] Al-Kayid firmly believed that the goals of the revolution would be weakened if operations against Israel were stopped.

The crisis was resolved on October 19 when al-Kayid and his lieutenant "Abu Zaim" agreed to be transferred to other positions. The crisis, however, resulted in the deaths of nine men, since fighting had broken out between the two Fatah factions.[i] This intra-Fatah rivalry did nothing to forward intergroup unity. It was as if the leader of the unity drive was unable to solve his own unity problems. The "committees" formed in April, therefore, reported back to the Executive Committee of their continuous failure to achieve unity among the groups.

The second major problem the Palestinian movement faced was dissention within Lebanon. Guerrilla operations from Lebanon into Israel had increased as a result of the closing of the Jordanian bases. As a result Israel repeatedly sent warnings of retaliation to the Lebanese government, holding it responsible for these guerrilla acts. These threats, in turn, forced the Lebanese government to review its own policy toward the guerrillas based in Lebanon.

In 1972 terrorism continued unabated. The Black September Organization no longer concentrated solely on Jordanian personnel and interests. Israel now became the principal target. In all the operations undertaken by the guerrillas, their objectives were, for the most part, clearly announced. Several terrorist operations were staged to obtain the release of prisoners. In others the reason given or strongly implied was punishment. Only one act in 1972 was staged for the purpose of obtaining ransom money.

During 1973 and 1974, the Palestinian guerrilla movement underwent considerable strain, both internal as well as external. On the international scene, terrorism continued unabated. However, the guerrilla organizations were involved primarily with their internal affairs.

The Palestinian movement was greatly affected by the October war. Prior to the opening of hostilities on October 6, the Arab states abutting on Israel resolved their differences[31] and presented a unified front to the enemy. The Palestinians, heretofore, had been supported by the Egyptians in their dispute with the Jordanian regime. They now found themselves shunted aside. After the war, they became even more isolated in the Arab world when they came out strongly in opposition to the ceasefire agreements. Later, however, Yasser Arafat began to press for the acceptance of peace maneuvers. He envisaged a role for the Palestinians at any international conference, which would be held to attempt to resolve

---

[i] The dispute was mediated successfully by the Algerian ambassador to Lebanon who had been asked by Arafat to use his good offices in the conflict. (See: *The Arab World*, October 20, 1972, p. 5.)

the Middle East dilemma. Fearful of total isolation in the Arab world where "peace" suddenly became an important word in the dialogues eminating from the Arab capitals, Arafat realized that the Palestinians should be willing to accept whatever fragment was offered to them of a rump Palestinian state. Total negativism would only cause bitterness with the Arab states that expended so much energy, material, manpower, and territory in the name of the Palestinian cause.

2 The Palestinian Revolutionary Movement

A continuous process of fragmentation and coalescence has characterized the development of the Palestinian revolutionary movement. Ten guerrilla groups come to represent virtually the entire revolutionary effort. All were brought into the Palestine Liberation Organization. The process of unification, however, has been long and turbulent.

After the PLO was discredited during the 1967 June war, the National Congress, which had not met since 1964, was reconvened in January 1968, and again in July 1968. At both meetings the guerrilla groups were represented by their delegates. Only as-Sa'iqa was excluded. Fatah now came to share control with the former members of the PLO. In February 1969, the National Congress was convened once more shortly after the PLA asserted its autonomy in the wake of a mutiny within its ranks over the appointment by Executive Committee of a new commander.[1] At this meeting the delegates now came to represent the guerrilla organizations (with the exception of the PFLP, which was splintering), the workers' unions, student organizations, women's organizations, and independents.[2] The membership of the Executive Committee was altered to reflect the eminence of Fatah. It was assigned 4 of the 11 seats of the Executive Committee, and Yasser Arafat, the spokesman for Fatah, was elected chairman. Two seats were assigned to Sa'iqa, 1 to a member of the former PLO, and 3 to independents.[3] The independents tended to lean towards Fatah, and, as such, Fatah consolidated its position within the PLO. The National Congress had been convened in an attempt to settle the differences between the PLO and the PLA, and to attempt to iron out the ideological differences between Fatah and the PFLP. Fatah had, in a sense, pressured for the convening of the National Congress, hoping thereby that a binding agreement could be arrived at. The National Congress refused to get involved, but with Sa'iqa in the fold some coalescence had been achieved. Subsequently, the PLA (composed of regulars and guerrilla units) was to rejoin the PLO, and the PLO Executive Committee expanded its functions to include an information center, a research center, and a planning center.[4]

Fatah's search for unity led to the creation of the Palestine Armed Struggle Command (PASC). The course of events leading to the creation of PASC is as follows:

19

In the course of these battles and victories, Fatah was calling for and working to achieve national unity. In early 1968, it convened the commando organizations to create the "Permanent Office for Commando Action" which comprised eight commando organizations. Fatah laid down a plan of action for this office. It developed it and many of the commando organizations merged in Fatah but the Palestine Liberation Organization (PLO) and the Popular Front for the Liberation of Palestine refused to join this office. Fatah subsequently attempted to create a new, acceptable form for national unity by developing the idea of a national front. But the PLO rejected the idea at the time on the grounds that it is the mother organization rather than one of the parties along with the other organizations. A short time thereafter Fatah suggested the PLO as a framework where all commando organizations could meet. The Fourth National Congress convened and made drastic changes in the PLO's national pact to reconcile it with the nature of the current phase of our national struggle. The National Congress decided to set up the Palestinian Armed Struggle Command (PASC) and national unity started to crystallize although some refrained from joining it. PASC now represents 97% of the Palestinian force.[5]

PASC was, therefore, created to improve cooperation in the military field, and circumvented the political or ideological differences. All of the guerrilla groups joined PASC with the exception of the PFLP. At the local level, however, at all border crossings and in the refugee camps, cooperation between PASC and members of the PFLP soon developed.

In February 1970, as a result of the crisis in Jordan between the Jordanian authorities and the Palestinian guerrillas, the Unified Command of Palestine Resistance (UCPR) was created. The UCPR included at this time all the guerrilla organizations, and was conceived to be a negotiating body that would represent the guerrilla groups in all crises which may arise with the Arab governments. Since the ideological differences that existed had prevented the PFLP from joining the PLO, the creation of the UCPR now provided the Palestinian guerrillas with an official body with which to confront the Arab governments. In essence, therefore, the Palestinians, pending a resolution of the ideological differences, achieved a degree of unity and the necessary organizations with which to face the Arabs and the Israelis.

By 1974 the PLO structure had been altered slightly, primarily to accommodate the numerous groups as well as to insure the continued supremacy of Fatah. The three main bodies of the organization—the Executive Committee, the National Council (formerly National Congress), and the PLA. However, the Executive Committee came to number 14, among whom were Yasser Arafat (Fatah), chairman; Faruq al-Qaddumi (Fatah), head of the Political Department; Zuhayr Muhsin (Sa'iqa), head of the Military Department; Muhammad Zuhdi an-Nashashibi (independent), secretary and head of the Administrative Affairs Department; Abd al-Aziz al-Wajih (PLA), deputy secretary; Hamid Abu Sittah (independent), head of the Occupied Homeland Department, Abd al-Jawad Salih (PNF),[a] deputy head of the Occupied Homeland Department and official in charge of the Executive Office for Home Affairs; Dr. Abd al-Wahab al-Kayyali (ALF), head of the Education and Cultural Affairs Department; and Abd al-Muhsin Abu Mayzar (PNF), official PLO spokesman and head of the National Pan-Arab and Returnees Affairs Department. Also on this committee are Adib Abd ar-Rabbuh (DPFLP) and clergyman Iliya Khoury, an independent from the West Bank.[b] This committee is responsible for the administration of the organization as well as for carrying out the directives of the National Council (formerly National Congress).[6]

Directly over the Executive Committee is the 31 member Central Council. Represented on this board are all the guerrilla organizations as well as independents and representatives from the West Bank and Gaza. This council was established to oversee the work of the Executive Committee and to feed to that same board politics and other statutes that govern the organization. It also hammers out the common philosophy of the PLO.

The National Council, now numbering 155 members, is the sounding board for the Palestinian people. Again, all groups are represented, including the guerrilla organizations, the West Bank groups, those living in occupied territories, and independents. It was originally set up to be held once a year to review policies and programs. However, for political reasons, sessions are held whenever it is feasible and when it appears opportune and advantageous for Arafat. Its power is extensive and is not a rubber stamp assembly for the Executive Committee or the Central Council.

The third maor division of the PLO is the Palestine Liberation Army (PLA). Currently headed by Brigadier General Misbah al-Budayri, this force has approximately 5,500 armed personnel. Its members are not a part of the guerrilla organizations. Instead they are drawn from the Palestinian populations who live primarily in Iraq, Syria, and Egypt. The PLA has its own commando branch, the Popular Liberation Forces (PLF), whose membership totals 1,100 and whose commander is Colonel Nihad Nusaybeh. The PLA is composed further of three brigades, the first of which is the Qadisiyah. It has approximately 1,200 men divided into three battalions. All are stationed in Syria. The Hittin Brigade (1,200) is sta-

[a] The Palestine National Front (PNF) is an organization composed of members residing or formerly residing in occupied territories. This is a different group from the one with the same name whose members are headquartered in Syria and whose aim is to continue the Palestinian revolution.

[b] Within the PLO are other departments whose members are not represented on the Executive Committee. These are the Palestine National Fund and the information branch (RASD). Also, since the withdrawal of the PFLP from the committee, the Popular Front organization has no representative at this time.

tioned in Syria and Lebanon. It, too, has three battalions. The third brigade, the Ayn Jallut, is stationed in Egypt and is integrated into the Egyptian armed forces structure. The latter two have recently been posted to Lebanon.

Within the PLO today, two factions have been trying to control policy of the movement. Arafat, considered by his peers to be moderate, has accepted the principle of peace and the establishment of a rump state within Palestine, possibly composed of the West Bank and Gaza.

Habash and his supporters, representatives of the ALF and the PFLP-GC, as well as his own PFLP, call moderates such as Arafat traitors to surrender to a policy of bowing to Arab governments bent on surrender.[7] Instead, the revolution must continue until the Israeli state disappears.

The moderate position had, in the past, called for a single state in which Arabs and Jews would live together, but without Zionism as a guiding principle. The Jews would evolve into a Mediterranean people and the two races would live in peace as they had in the past. Now, according to the pressure from the Arab states, the moderates are accepting the idea of two states in Palestine—one Arab and one Jewish.[8] As late as 19 June 1974, however, the PLO National Council voted to continue the struggle. The following points were approved at the June Cairo Conference of the Palestine National Council:

1. The assertion of the PLO position regarding Resolution 242 is that it obliterates the patriotic *(wataniyah)* and national *(qawmiyah)* rights of our people and deals with our people's cause as a refugee problem. Therefore, dealing with this resolution on this basis is rejected on any level of Arab and international dealings, including the Geneva conference.

2. The PLO will struggle by all means, foremost of which is armed struggle, to liberate Palestinian land and to establish the people's national, independent and fighting authority on every part of Palestinian land to be liberated. This necessitates making more changes in the balance of power in favor of our people and their struggle.

3. The PLO will struggle against any plan for the establishment of a Palestinian entity the price of which is recognition, conciliation, secure borders, renunciation of the national right, and our people's deprivation of their right to return and their right to determine their fate on their national soil.

4. Any liberation step that is achieved constitutes a step for continuing (the effort) to achieve the PLO strategy for the establishment of the Palestinian democratic state that is stipulated in the resolutions of the previous national councils.

5. To struggle with the Jordanian national forces for the establishment

of a Jordanian-Palestinian national front whose aim is the establishment of a national democratic government in Jordan—a government
that will cohere with the Palestinian entity to be established as a result of the struggle.

6. The PLO will strive to establish a unity of struggle between the two
   peoples (Palestinian and Jordanian peoples) and among all the Arab
   liberation movement forces that agree on this program.

7. In the light of this program, the PLO will struggle to strengthen national unity and to eliminate it to a level that will enable it to carry out
   its duties and its patriotic *(wataniyah)* and national *(qawmiyah)* tasks.

8. The Palestinian national authority, after its establishment, will struggle for the unity of the confrontation states for the sake of completing
   the liberation of all Palestinian soil and as a step on the path of comprehensive Arab unity.

9. The PLO will struggle to strengthen its solidarity with the socialist
   countries and the world forces of liberation and progress to foil all
   Zionist, reactionary and imperialist schemes.

10. In the light of this program, the revolution command will work out the
    tactics that will serve and lead to the achievement of these aims.

Nayif Hawatmeh was the first to come out for the two-state proposal.[9]
Although considered a radical, with strong Marxist leanings, he believes
that socialism will eventually be the saving grace for both populations and
under its banner, a unified socialist state will emerge.

This means that what the two sides will use to achieve their aims will
again vary greatly. The moderates favor peaceful maneuvers; the radicals, military means. Arafat, denied a mandate by the Palestinian leadership in 1975 to attend the then-anticipated Geneva conference, will nevertheless press for a Palestinian presence at any future international conference that will be held to resolve the Palestinian question. He will also be
forced to seek an accommodation with the Jordanian government, since
half the Palestinian masses remain under Jordanian control. Accommodation, however, with Jordan will mean the annulling of a policy to bring
down the Jordanian regime. Ever since the suppression of guerrilla forces
in Jordan in 1970 and 1971, the Palestinian groups have been calling for
the overthrow of King Hussein. Over half the Jordanian citizenry are Palestinians. Yet as long as the army retains power, the population has no
real voice in government processes. Family ties link the East Bank with
the West Bank. Yet they remain two separate people. If the moderates
come to terms with the Jordanian regime, their hand will be greatly
strengthened by the support the Jordanian Palestinian populace would
give them. If both sides remain opposed to one another, the Palestinian
movement will be weakened. The radicals continue to favor the over-

throw of the monarchy, which immediately prevents discussions, and, therefore, a chance to ameliorate the Palestinians' plight.

The situation is further complicated by the emergence of a political bloc in the occupied areas. This group supports Arafat and the PLO as being the sole representatives of the Palestinian people. It also favors peace and the establishment of a rump Palestinian state. But what of those Palestinians who live in Syria and Lebanon? Their attitude is again different. They are reluctant to see established a rump state; the majority of them are not from the West Bank or Gaza but from Israel proper. They will not have ties to a new Palestinian state unless it will comprise the entire Palestine area. Yet they no longer support fully the use of arms to liberate their country; instead they would rather harken back to the moderates' stand of last year in which a single state will be created and whose population will be both Jews and Arabs.

Although the radical groups have favored the use of terrorism, even al-Fatah has used extranormal acts of violence to better its position in the Arab community. Since first initiated in 1968, the number of terrorist acts have continued to mount. The reasons vary per group or act. Some operations are staged to tell the world there is a Palestinian entity. Others are shown to be acts of vengeance. Still others are mounted to gain prestige within the Palestinian movement. The latest terrorist acts committed by Ahmad Jabril's group were meant to disrupt peace negotiations.

Whatever the reason, as a weapon, terrorism has been successful in keeping the Palestinian cause before the world community. Those members belonging to the "Rejection Front"—PFLP, Arab Liberation Front (ALF), PFLP-GC, and the Popular Revolutionary Front (PRFLP)—have stated categorically they will refuse to negotiate, and they will continue to use military means to resolve the Palestine issue.

If peace negotiations do not result in an acceptable and concrete solution to the Palestine question, there will be no alternative for the moderates but to revive their "fight and talk" tactics. Although, it has been announced that al-Fatah will direct its operations solely inside Israel, it may change its scenario to the international arena. How long the moderates will be able to restrain the radicals is a debatable point. As it stands now, they will continue to put pressure on Israel by all means in order to force the issue. However, they may be forced to use stronger tactics if negotiations drag on interminably.

PLO Guerrilla Organizations

A brief summary of each of the guerrilla groups within the PLO follows:

Al Fatah[c]

Composed of approximately 5,000 active members and 15,000 reserves, al-Fatah is the largest group in the Palestinian movement. Founded in the 1950s by Arafat and some close associates, it soon became known through its publication, *Our Palestine*. It was the first Palestinian organization to believe in the principle of self-help, whereby the Palestinians, and not the Arab states, should be responsible for their destiny. The first military operations against Israel took place in 1965 and were to escalate in the ensuing years. After the battle of Karameh (March 1968) during which al-Fatah members were very conspicuous, the ranks were swelled by volunteers clamoring to enlist in the organization. Arafat became head of the PLO, increasing his prestige within the Arab world. He was, in fact, accorded the status of head of state at inter-Arab conferences in which he participated.

The increase of Fatah's regular forces compelled the organization to establish a complex system of administration. A central committee was formed among the founders of the group. Approximately 10 in number, these men carry out the wishes of the general congress and oversee the administrative activities of the organization. The General Congress usually meets once a year to elect members to the Central Committee and the Revolutionary Council as well as to determine the course of action the organization is supposed to take during the coming year. Real power is held by the Revolutionary Council, however, whose 33 members are responsible for determining policy and for making momentous decisions. Al-Asifah, the paramilitary wing of the organization, undertakes military activities of the group. Smaller committees or branches within Fatah have other specific duties. For example, the External Security Branch maintains security operations for the leaders of the organization. RASD (Jihaz al-Rasd) is the intelligence gathering service, with numerous offices abroad. And the Foreign Relations Branch supervises control of the operational cells located in many countries throughout the world.

Fatah is not only involved in guerrilla operations; it maintains social service branches that function as public health installations, field hospitals, orphanages, and schools. It also distributes funds to the families of members who were killed in the line of duty or who are currently imprisoned by the Israelis.

Although Arafat retains control of the entire organization, there are three factions that, unless rigidly controlled, could split the rank and file

---

[c] Its name is officially Harakat al-Tahrir al-Filastiniya (the Movement for the Liberation of Palestine). Fatah is derived from the first letters of the three words, but in reverse order.

of the group.[10] One is subservient to Arafat. The second is headed by Sa-lah Khalaf of Black September fame, who is considered to be an oppor-tunist, yet will bide his time until the moment when Arafat faulters. The third group has leftist tendencies and is considered to be more militant than Arafat's group.

Popular Front for the Liberation of Palestine (PFLP)

Composed of approximately 2,000 members, PFLP's dedicated active core numbers only 500. The organization was founded by George Habash and Nayif Hawatmeh as a breakaway group of the Arab Nationalist Movement (ANM). Emerging in December 1967, as a result of the union of two other splinter groups (Vengeance Youth and the Palestine Liber-ation Front), the PFLP concentrated on urban sabotage and terrorist ac-tivities. Its most famous coup occurred in 1970 with the hijacking of sev-eral planes to Jordan, acts that precipitated the Jordanian attack on guer-rilla positions.

The organization is structured into three major departments: the Po-litical Bureau, the Military Command, and the Administrative Command. There exists also a Central Committee, composed of the leaders of the three departments whose object is to define and supervise policy for the organization.

Because of its stress on ideology, the Political Bureau assumes the most important role in the organization. Its members are the leading per-sonnel of the group—dedicated Marxists bent on converting the Palestin-ian masses to their ideological thinking. Politicies are channeled to cell leaders who, in turn, relate the directives to their cadre. Because of its leftist dogma, the PFLP has the closest contacts with other leftist interna-tional radical groups, such as the Red Army of Japan and the Baader-Meinhoff group in West Germany.

Its leftist doctrines have been the main reason why funds from most Arab governments have not been forthcoming. Communism is anathema to the peninsula countries as well as to Libya. Only Iraq has provided suf-ficient funds to enable the organization to remain solvent. When these were not forthcoming, hijacking for ransom was used. Furthermore, since Habash and other PFLP leaders are Christians, the non-Marxist Muslim, desirous of joining a commando group, would gravitate toward other or-ganizations. Its appeal, then, is limited. One of the main reasons, thus, for staging the spectacular attacks against international aviation was to gain favor with the Muslim masses. The doctrinaire approach of the organiza-tion is also responsible for the rifts that have taken place in the ranks of the PFLP membership. Even today, dissension continues between those who support Habash and those who surround the more radical elements, such as Wadi Haddad and his cousin, Marwan Haddad.

*Popular Democratic Front for the Liberation of Palestine
(DPFLP)*

Composed of a small core of approximately 100, with approximately 1,200 adherents, DPFLP, founded by Nayif Hawatmeh, is a spin-off from the PFLP. Created in February 1969, following bitter disputes between Habash and Hawatmeh, the organization has stressed from the start the Marxist-Leninist dogma to its recruits. It began operations one month later.

Structurally it is similar to the PFLP, in that the Political Bureau holds most of the power in the organization. A Central Committee, composed of the elite members of the Political Bureau, directs the administrative functions of the group, as well as the military operations.

Sa'iqa

Sa'iqa, officially entitled the Vanguard of the Popular Liberation War, was created in 1968. Its membership totals about 5,000, and is closely linked to the Syrian government. In fact, it has been equipped and financed primarily by the Damascus regimes. Led by Zuhayr Muhsin, a Syrian Ba'thi, it is a strong paramilitary group. The organization, as such, is structured with two major departments: political and military.[d] Its activities have been contained, however, by the Syrian government. To date, its main function has been to act as an adjunct of Syrian policy. For example, it participated in the Jordanian strife of 1970-71 as part of the force sent by Syria into Jordan. Furthermore, it was used to support the hard-pressed guerrillas in the 1969 clashes in Lebanon. Currently it is being used in Lebanon.

Normally, its forces have been confined to camps designated by the Syrian army. As such, the Syrians have prevented border incursions from taking place. Yet, Sa'iqa remains an effective paramilitary fighting force, highly trained, well equipped, and a potential danger to those who oppose the Syrian government, as seen in the recent fighting in Lebanon.

*Popular Front for the Liberation of Palestine-General
Command (PFLP-GC)*

PFLP-GC is small, commanding no more than 300 highly trained personnel. Its leader is Ahmad Jabril, a former PFLP member who left that group after a dispute with its leadership regarding ideology. Jabril is con-

---

[d] There are four battalions under the military section, each one composed of from 3 to 600 men.

sidered to be one of the best military strategists in the Palestinian movement.

The PFLP-GC has tended to restict its operations to forays inside Israel. Three known exceptions did take place, however, all involving the destruction of planes. Jabril has promised many more operations though, thereby proving himself to be the most dangerous Palestinian guerrilla leader and the greatest potential disrupter of current peace negotiations. Now that his group has been brought into the PLO, there is a chance that Arafat may be able to curtail his terrorist operations. But it is doubtful whether an indefinite postponement of operations could be achieved.

Arab Liberation Forces (ALF)

This group, perhaps the most ineffective of all the commando organizations, has a membership of between 150 and 500. Its sponsor is the Iraqi government, whose Ba'thi leaders keep strict control over its activities. The ALF was founded in 1969 as a result of the Iraqi Ba'thi quarrels with the Fatah leadership. Also involved was an attempt to emulate the Syrians who had recently established Sa'iqa. Its main function has been to act as a sounding board for Iraqi propaganda. For this reason it is pitted against Syrian backed Palestinian forces in the fighting in Lebanon.

Arab Organization for the Liberation of Palestine (AOLP)

Like the other small guerrilla groups, AOLP's membership numbers no more than 300. Its leader, Dr. Isam al-Sartawi, had attempted to work with Fatah, but decided to form his own group in February 1969. Although still retaining autonomy, it has virtually become a part of Fatah, primarily because of the decimation of its ranks during the Jordanian strife and second, because Fatah, as the leading guerrilla organization within the PLO, is able to disburse its largesses to those who support it.

Palestine Popular Struggle Front (PSF)

PSF, although small in number (200-500), has been active both inside Israel and on the international scene. Bahjat Abu Ghabiyya, present leader of the group, founded the PSF in early 1968. Because he was a former PLO Executive Council member, he was and is well respected. Although his group did not represent any important segment of the Palestinian movement, the PSF was supported by larger groups as a possible ally or as a spokesman for their own positions.[11]

Al-Ansar

Communist supported, al-Ansar is a small organization that exists solely for political use by the Communist parties in the various Arab countries. Although established in 1970, it was only recently (1973) that the PLO member organizations permitted a representative to join the National Congress sessions.

Popular Revoutionary Front for the Liberation of Palestine (PRFLP)

This group is composed of men steeped in Marxist-Leninist dogma. The founders broke from the PFLP in March 1972, yet are attempting to work with that group within the "Rejection Front." The leader of the group is Muhammad al-Farhan who keeps a tight reign over his forces. Their operations to date have been few.

Palestine National Front (PNF)

This organization is composed of a group of young Palestinians who are opposed to Arafat's policy to seek a solution of the Palestinian problem through peaceful means. Almost all of its 400 recruits come from the West Bank and have now settled in the Yarmuk Camp near Damascus, Syria. The leaders are Muhammad Sulayman Haju, Arif al-Maw'id, and Nabil al-Salti. Because of close supervision by the Syrian government, this group has not engaged in any terrorist operations as yet.

The Rejection Front

Mention was made of the Rejection Front when discussing the PRFLP. This loosely knit conglomeration is composed of the PFLP, PFLP-GC, ALF, and PRFLP. Their one common bond is opposition to Arafat and his plans for a peaceful solution to Middle East strife. Both the PFLP and the ALF have withdrawn in protest from the Executive Committee of the PLO to show their displeasure at the policies favored by the majority. Although there exists a potential threat to Arafat's leadership from the Rejection Front members, the strong personalities, though, of the Front leaders tend to prevent the formulation of unified plans.

Ideological Differences among the Guerrilla Organizations

The basic ideological and tactical differences that have affected relationships between Fatah, on the one hand, and the PFLP and DPFLP on the other, deal with: the purposes of the Palestinian revolution during the liberation and postliberation phases; the approaches and methods to be adopted during these two phases; and the tactics employed to achieve the desired effect.

Fatah, the PFLP, and the DPFLP share in the belief that the Palestinian revolution is part of a worldwide liberation movement against colonialism, imperialism, and Zionism. They further believe that the Palestinian revolution should join with other revolutionary movements in a broadbased united front, where cooperation and the coordination of efforts against the common enemy can be accomplished.[12] As far as the Palestinian struggle against Israel and Zionism is concerned, all three reject classical warfare as an alternative to "a people's war." Fatah, however, rejects the need for ideological commitment as a necessary precondition to launching a "people's war."

At a meeting at the American University of Beirut, the position of Fatah was partially explained by one of its spokesmen, Abu Iyad (Salah Khalaf), considered by many to be the second highest-ranking spokesman for Fatah, who stated;

There were no points of view—from the extreme Right to the extreme Left—that we did not share, in the hope of regaining Palestine; and the result was bitter disappointment. . . .

. . . We used to say that Zionism could not be fought along military classical lines, but rather through an all encompassing war of popular liberation. This hidden conflict between us and the Arab regimes continued until the June war which proved the failure of both leftist and rightist policies. For had our masses in the West Bank, Sinai, and Golan been armed, the Israeli army could not have penetrated and conquered these areas.[13]

The position of Fatah is further clarified in the following statement:

Q. Some of the combatant Palestinian organizations have proposed for themselves a specific ideology based on Marxist-Leninist foundations. What is Fatah's position towards this idealogy?

A. I fear that our rejection of this proposal will be construed as enmity towards some for the socialist countries which stand by us in our struggle and fight. And I hope that it will be understood by all that we bear no ill-feeling to these friendly nations which have supported us, and support us still, on most positions, especially our brothers in the Peoples Republic of China. When we criticize this proposal it does not mean that we are criticizing these friendly nations. . . . These nations cannot, in any way, be equated with international imperialism. But, at the same time, we say that the presentation of this proposal at this stage does not conform to Marxism and Leninism. . . .

We say it without ambiguity that we are in the midst of a national liberation revolution, and not a social revolution. Thus it must be clear to, and understood by all that we do not oppose the idea [specific ideology based on Marxism-Leninism], or whatever is proposed from an objective point of view, but we oppose the manner in which it is presented and the timing of the presentation.[e]

In essence, therefore, Fatah rejects any ideological interpretation that may be imputed to the Palestinian revolution at this stage of its development, and chooses, instead, to emphasize only its nationalist, anti-Zionist and anti-imperialist character. This insistence on an ideologically neutral, nationalist movement is further reflected in the belief that "the struggle for Palestine must be a strictly Palestinian undertaking,"[14] and Fatah's unwillingness to interfere in the affairs of, or be drawn into squabbles with, Arab states.

The overall position of Fatah is based on a pragmatic evaluation of the environment in which the Palestinian revolution must operate, and, of necessity, recognize by "remaining aloof from the ideological currents, commitments or styles prevailing in the Arab world, or blowing in from the outside."[15] Fatah, in fact, was able to rise above the ideological dissensions that have split the Arab world, and was supported by the people as well as the governments of the Arab world. Fatah's refusal to adhere to any ideology while insisting that the liberation of Palestine was the task of Palestinians only enabled it to provide a message to the Palestinian community of remarkable simplicity and clarity—a fact that may partially explain its success with the masses.[f]

In its attempts to remain ideologically neutral and yet reach a basis of understanding with ideologically committed Palestinian guerrilla groups, develop a political platform that may appeal to a specific Israeli audience, and avoid the antagonism of host Arab governments, Fatah faces a number of dilemmas. These relate to the kind of sociopolitical structure that will be establsihed in a liberated Palestine, the fate of the Israelis once liberation is accomplished, and the international boundaries of such a state.

At first, Fatah avoided the issue and stated simply that the sociopolitical composition of the state would reflect the ideological orientation of the liberators. Later Fatah modified its position by stating that

A democratic and progressive Palestine, however, rejects by elimination a theo-

---

[e] "We are in the Midst of a National Liberation Revolution and not a Social Revolution," *Fatah* (Arabic version), January 26, 1970, p. 5.

[f] "To the Palestinians, in the most simple terms, it proclaims that (1) the conflict is between Israelis and Palestinians, not Israelis and Arabs, (2) that the Palestinians have an unshakable right to bear arms against Israel ('Our cause is just'), and (3) that 'we may not see victory, our sons may not see victory, but our son's sons will carry on the fight,' (words spoken by Abu Amar in an interview with an NBC television reporter)." Wilson. *Palestinian Guerrilla Movements*, p. 48.

cratic, a feudalist, an aristocratic, and an authoritarian or a racist-chauvinistic form of government. It will be a country that does not allow oppression or exploitation of any group or people by any other group or individuals; a state that provides equal opportunities for its people in work, worship, education, political decision-making, cultural and artistic expression.[16]

Similarly, the position of Fatah as it relates to the Jewish constituents of a liberated Palestine has evolved to the point that it now clashes with Article 6 of the ten-year-old Palestine National Covenant. Article 6 states that Jews who had lived in Palestine prior to the establishment of the Israeli state in 1948 are Palestinians.[17] Fatah rejects the above article because it precludes all the Jewish immigrants who came to, or were born in, Palestine since 1948, and because it includes a category of Israeli citizens who will not qualify.

Equally, this means that all Jewish Palestinians—at the present Israelis—have the same right provided of course that they reject Zionist racist chauvinism and fully accept to live as Palestinians in the New Palestine. The revolution therefore rejects the supposition that only Jews who lived in Palestine prior to 1948 or prior to 1914 and their descendents are acceptable. After all Dayan and Allon were born in Palestine before 1948 and they—with many of their colleagues—are diehard racist Zionists who obviously do not qualify for a Palestinian status. Whereas newcomers may be anti-Zionists and work ardently for the creation of the new Palestine.[18]

Article 2 of the Palestine National Covenant states that Palestine constitutes the land that existed during the British Mandate under the geographic name of Palestine. Fatah referred to Palestine under the British Mandate as that territory to be liberated, and acknowledged the possibility of contention over Jordan's annexation of the West Bank.

In 1974 this interpretation changed drastically when Arafat accepted the idea that a Palestinian state could be formed from part of the land called Palestine under the British Mandate. Here lies the basic area of contention between the two major factions within the guerrilla movement.

The PFLP and the DPFLP represent the two most radical and articulate guerrilla groups among the "universalists." The DPFLP broke away from the PFLP, but both espouse Marxist-Leninist ideologies. The differences between them are a matter of degree and not substance. Nayif Hawatmeh, the leader of the DPFLP, an ardent admirer of Mao Tse-tung, considers the Soviet Communist party not to be revolutionary, and believes Fatah to be a bourgeois government apparatus.[19]

According to the PFLP, Israel's technical superiority and the quantitative armament balance between Israel and the Arab states—a balance that both the East and the West seek to preserve—render conventional warfare, as a means by which the Arab states can defeat Israel, an impossible undertaking. It is only by adopting the concept of protracted warfare, in which the Arab human potential can be modernized, mobilized, and organized, that the Arabs will be insured of the upper hand. The modernization, mobilization, and organization of Arab society will be undertaken by a revolutionary Marxist-Leninist party using the principles of scientific socialism.

The PFLP posits Marxist-Leninist ideological commitment as the necessary prerequisite to launching a successful people's war. It rejects the basic nationalist approach of Fatah—that the conflict is between Israelis and Palestinians only—and views the Palestinian liberation effort as part of a greater national effort to liberate the Arab world from "world Zionism," "imperialism," and "Arab reaction." Cooperation with all national classes willing to participate in the liberation process is implied, although the PFLP holds that only the masses, that is, the peasants, the urban workers and the refugees, would be able to "convert guerrilla war into a people's war. . . ."[g]

Noninterference in the internal affairs of Arab states is predicated on the willingness of these states not to disrupt or impede the revolutionary effort. Arab governments that have sought to limit the activities of the Palestinians have been branded as counterrevolutionary. In spite of the well-publicized hostility of the PFLP towards these governments, it has, nonetheless followed Fatah's example and has adopted a cooperative posture.[20]

The DPFLP, on the other hand, takes the position that efforts at liberating Palestine cannot, at this stage, lead to meaningful results. These efforts must be preceeded by the overthrow of Arab governments and the radicalization of the Arab masses. A people's war, which places its reliance on the proletarian class—a class that has nothing to lose by bearing arms and fighting to the end, and everything to gain—will then be launched, in which a revolutionary Communist party will play a principal role.[21] As such, the DPFLP has not been involved, to any degree, in the guerrilla activities of the other Palestinian groups.

As far as Israel, the fate of the Israelis, and the sociopolitical composition and boundaries of a liberated Palestine are concerned, both the PFLP and the DPFLP hold that: (1) the continued existence of Israel is important until Arab societies are transformed into Marxist societies; (2) the Arab-Israeli conflict is, in essence, a class struggle between the Jewish and Arab proletarian class on the one hand, and the capitalist and imperi-

---

[g] Hisham Sharabi, *Palestine Guerrillas: Their Credibility and Effectiveness* (Washington, D.C.: Georgetown University, 1970), p. 26. It is interesting to note that the PFLP considers reaction and petty bourgeoisie to be officially established in Egypt, Algeria, and Syria, and to a lesser extent in Iraq. (See *an-Nahar* (Sunday Supplement), March 22, 1970, p. 4). George Habash, the leader of the PFLP, was arrested by the Syrian authorities in August 1968, and at the time of the arrest the Front became publicly critical of the Syrian Regime.

alist forces on the other, including Arab capitalism and the Arab classes that cooperate with the West and that are thereby equated with Zionism;[h] and (3) the boundary disputes will be easily resolved by Marxist societies. The DPFLP, in fact, called for the initiation of a dialogue with progressive Israeli organizations, on the basis of a common struggle that will unite all the progressive democratic forces in the area, especially those in the ranks of the Palestinian resistance, the Israeli society, and the progressive Jews.[22]

Strategic and Tactical Differences

The nationalist stance of Fatah and the Marxist-Leninist ideology of the PFLP are reflected in the strategies and tactics adopted by them. In the context of the Palestinian revolution, Fatah seeks to promote unity among the guerrilla groups, regardless of ideological differences and without the application of force, in some sort of collegium. In the context of the Arab world, Fatah seeks the financial and diplomatic support of Arab states irrespective of their political orientation. As far as Jordan, Syria, Lebanon, and, to a lesser extent, Egypt—the countries that have common borders with Israel and borders the guerrilla organizations must have access to in order to continue their efforts—are concerned, Fatah continuously seeks to reconcile the interests of these states and the interests of the Palestinian revolution. It has, on many occasions, moved to prevent a situation that confronted a Palestinian guerrilla group and an Arab government from escalating into open warfare. As such, it has played an instrumental role in bringing about such agreements as the Cairo Accord.[i] Yasser Arafat, as chairman of the Executive Committee of the PLO, has attended Arab summit meetings and visited a number of Arab heads of state to present the Palestinian point of view and to smooth over any differences that may have arisen.

In the Islamic milieu, Fatah has sought to gain recognition and support, for itself and the Palestinian revolution, by attending Islamic summit meetings and the meetings of the foreign ministers of Islamic states.

---

[h] The position of the PFLP and DPFLP via-à-vis Israel differs little from the position taken by the Communist parties of Lebanon and Syria. From 1936 onward, these Communist parties have: (1) made a distinction between Jews and Zionists; (2) have held that Zionism was a racist, capitalist, and imperialist movement; and (3) have held that a class-struggle between the Jewish and Arab proletariat, on the one hand, and Zionism and Arab capitalism, on the other, was at the root of the Arab-Israeli conflict. For more information, see: Sami (Khoury) Ayoub, *Al-Hisb al-Shuyu'e fi Suriya wa Lubnan (The Communist Party in Syria and Lebanon: 1922-1958)* (Beirut Printing and Publishing House, 1959), pp. 87, 88, 143-51, 170-73.

[i] An agreement between the Lebanese government and representatives of the Palestine Liberation Organization, during the October-November 1969 crisis, in which guerrilla activity in Lebanon, and across Lebanon's border was reconciled with Lebanon's national interest.

In the international arena, Fatah seeks recognition and support from any country, East or West, by publicizing the Palestinian case through information bureaus. It combats Zionism by accepting invitations to participate in discussions of the Arab-Israeli conflict sponsored by student organizations, labor unions, and political parties.

Conscious of its present strength and the environment in which it lives and operates, Fatah, in its military activities against Israel, has resorted to a policy of limited confrontation[23] for the following reasons: (1) Fatah cannot hope to defeat Israel alone. Its military activities therefore must strike at the fringes of Israeli power in the hopes of creating an adverse psychological climate in Israel and a positive psychological climate in the Arab world. (2) Military operations against Israel must not be of the type that would provoke major reprisal raids against the Arab countries from which these operations are launched. Major Israeli reprisal raids can, in the absence of a mobilized Arab society, adversely affect the relationships of Fatah and the Arab states affected. (3) Palestinians living in the occupied territories are being used in very limited roles to avoid severe repressionary measures by the Israeli authorities. These measures may exacerbate the refugee problem by engendering further migration, when the continued presence of the Palestinians in the occupied areas is imperative if vacated lands are to be denied to the Israelis, and the claim to an Arab Palestine maintained. Passive resistance and noncooperation— strikes and demonstrations—are stressed to prevent the incorporation of the Palestinians by the Israelis in a Greater Israel.[24] (4) Attacks on Israeli properties and personnel—hijacking of airplanes, bombing of embassies and commercial interests, and the shooting of officials and personnel— located in foreign states are forbidden so as not to embarrass friendly nations and to avoid international approbation that would hamper Fatah's efforts to secure international recognition.[25]

The PFLP, on the other hand, chooses to wage total war against Israel, Zionism, Arab reaction, and imperialism. Its strategy and tactics are influenced by its ideology and by its limited resources and small following.[j] In pursuing its aim of liberation in the Arab world, it has not remained aloof from involvement in the internal affairs of Arab states: supporting Marxist-Leninist movements, especially in the Arabian Peninsula, and blowing up, or threatening to blow up, the Trans-Arabian pipeline, which affects the economies of Saudi Arabia, Jordan, Syria, and Lebanon.

---

[j]It should be noted that the PFLP does not receive the financial support Fatah elicits from Arab governments and Palestinians; and, as such, it is limited in the number of weapons it can purchase and the standing force it can maintain. This, in turn, limits the number of raids it can launch, and forces the Front to rely on cheaper, but just as effective, urban sabotage. The Front's ideology, on the other hand, attracts the Arab intellectuals but is too complicated for the masses.

The Front's activities in Israel and the occupied territories concentrate heavily on urban sabotage against Israeli and Palestinian targets alike. The use of urban sabotage against Israeli targets is partly related to the waging of total war; for the guerrillas feel justified in striking against civilian targets since Israel uses its weapons to kill civilians in its retaliation for guerrilla raids.[26] It is also based on a desire to create an atmosphere of distrust so complete that cooperation between Israelis and Palestinians, and the integration of the Palestinians into a Greater Israel, become impossible. The use of sabotage against Israeli targets results, generally, in the application of severe repressionary measures against the Palestinians; and the ensuing resentment contributes further to the climate of suspicion and noncooperation. Likewise, sabotage against Palestinian targets aims at punishing those who cooperate with the Israeli authorities, and serves to deter those who may contemplate cooperation in the future.[k]

In pursuance of its campaign against the overseas interests of Israel, the PFLP has resorted to the hijacking and bombing of Israeli airplanes,[l] and the bombing of Israeli embassies, and airline and shipping offices. British commercial establishments, belonging to British Jews accused by the Front of supporting Israel, also have beem bombed or threatened with bombing. Even the hijacking of American civilian airplanes and the bombings of American interests in Lebanon and elsewhere are considered a part of the PFLP's warfare against Zionism and imperialism for the support given to Israel by the United States.[m]

The Universalists and the Institutionalized

The two major institutionalized guerrilla groups are the as-Sa'iqa (affiliated with the Syrian wing of the Ba'th party), and the Arab Liberation Front (affiliated with the Iraqi wing of the Ba'th party). The differences

[k] The Arab mayor of Hebron, Muhammad Ali Jaabari, gave up in his attempts to create an autonomous regime in the West Bank as a result of Israeli government inaction, and after threats on his life were made by the Palestinian guerrillas. See: "Egyptian Missile Sites Attacked by Israeli Jets," *Washington Post*, April 1, 1970, p. A17.

[l] El Al Airlines is considered to be a military transport airline by the PFLP because of the role El Al played during the 1967 and 1973 wars, and because it continues to freight military equipment.

[m] According to the PFLP the bombing of American-owned—private and government—installations was in retaliation for the U.S. Embassy's efforts to foment religious strife in Lebanon. Subsequently, the Higher Political Committee For Palestinians—a loose organization that coordinates the political activities of the guerrilla groups in Lebanon, including that of the PFLP—issued a statement calling the bombings irresponsible. (See: "The Higher Committee for the Palestinians Accuses the Popular Front of Serving the Imperialist Designs," *An-Nahar*, March 31, 1970, pp. 1 and 10.)

that exist between the universalists and the institutionalized guerrilla groups are philosophical and ideological.

The universalists reject control by, and affiliation with, any Arab government. The universalists insist that dependence on, and affiliation with, Arab governments will immobilize the Palestinian revolution—as was the case between 1948 and 1967—and transform it into a tool of the foreign policies of these states. Fatah fears that the nationalist character of the Palestinian revolution will be subordinated to the Arab socialist ideology of the Ba'th parties, while the PFLP and DPFLP will not entrust the Palestinian revolution to Arab governments they consider either reactionary or petty bourgeois.

The institutionalization of Sa'iqa and the ALF by the Syrian and Iraqi wings of the Ba'th party stems from: (1) a willingness to show that the Ba'th could "adapt to needs of revolutionary warfare,"[27] (2) a requirement to maintain governmental authority, and (3) a clash in ideological emphasis.

The defeat of the Arab armies in the June 1967 war, and the subsequent inability of these armies to meet the Israeli threat, affected the prestige the Arab armies enjoyed prior to 1967, and weakened the authority of the Arab governments, which had placed great hope in their armies and the concept of classical warfare. The emergence of the guerrilla, moreover, as a new phenomenon capable of captivating the imagination and loyalty of the Arab intellectuals and masses, gave credence to the concept of guerrilla warfare as a means of defeating Israel. To many Arabs, he has become more than a hero. Instead, he is a new breed of Arab, free from both Israeli and Arab governmental domination.[28]

The growth and popularity the Palestinian guerrillas enjoyed, and the freedom of action and movement they demanded necessitated the imposition of controls[n] that would not appear to be antiguerrilla. The recruitment of Syrian and Iraqi nationals by the Palestinian guerrillas could, if unchecked, subvert governmental authority, and guerrilla raids against Israel would, if launched without government approval, commit governments to a specific policy and deprive them of other options.

The Syrian and Iraqi wings of the Ba'th party eschew an ideology that, as it relates to guerrilla action, holds that the primary purpose of such action is to bring change to the existing regimes in the Arab world. Both wings have sought to promote this political aspect, and, therefore, have come into conflict with the nationalist stance and unwillingness of Fatah to become involved in inter-Arab rivalries, and with the Marxist-Leninist

---

[n] "The Communist *al Nida'* reported Iraqi controls over Palestinian commando groups including the requests that the groups in Iraq work through the Iraqi-controlled Arab Liberation Front and that the groups maintain contact with the government on military and information matters." (See *The Middle East Journal* 23, no. 3, Summer 1969, p. 366.)

ideology of the PFLP and DPFLP as well. By virtue of the membership of as-Sa'iqa and the ALF in the PLO, the Syrian and Iraqi governments demonstrated their willingness to support the Palestinian revolution, yet, showed their ability to adapt to the needs of revolutionary warfare. By requiring the Palestinian guerrilla groups to work through as-Sa'iqa and the AFL when on Syrian and Iraqi soil, these governments, in fact, retained their authority, and by being able to station as-Sa'iqa and AFL forces on the territory of other Arab governments, they have been able to pursue their ideological goals by participation in, and support of, the Palestinian revolution.

The Communist Guerrilla Group

The decision of the Communist parties of Jordan, Syria, Iraq, and Lebanon to constitute a Communist guerrilla group, al-Ansar (the partisans), and have it seek membership in the PLO ranks is fraught with implications. The PFLP had repeatedly criticized the Arab Communist parties for their aloofness and lack of support; and the decision, therefore, could have been a reaction to that criticism. However, it coincides with a noticeable change in the attitude of the Soviet Union toward the Palestinian guerrillas, and comes in the wake of a visit made to the Soviet Union on 10 February 1970 by Yasser Arafat and other members of the PLO. The decision also preceded the visit of Yasser Arafat to the People's Republics of China and North Vietnam, which took place on the 21st of March 1970. If the Communist parties in Syria, Jordan, Iraq, and Lebanon acted on a signal from the Soviet Communist party, then the Soviet decision to support the Palestinian Revolution could be the result of the following: (1) an assessment of the relative strengths of the Arab governments and the Palestinian revolution; (2) reaction to criticisms leveled at the Soviet Union by the People's Republic of China, and worry about the increasing Chinese Communist penetration of the Arab world; (3) a desire to control the Palestinian revolution through the Communist guerrilla group; and (4) a combination of the above.

For the Palestinian guerrilla groups, the decision of the Communist parties of Jordan, Syria, Iraq, and Lebanon represents a turning point. For Fatah, the PFLP, and the DPFLP it represents the beginning of a much desired cooperation. For the PFLP and DPFLP it is the manifestation of the solidarity of the Marxist-Leninist camp; and for the Palestinians as a nation, it represents the commitment of a large number of non-Palestinian Arabs to their cause. Any attempt, however, by the Communists to control the Palestinian revolution will create dissension. For that matter, action taken by any other political party—the Muslim Brotherhood, the Syrian Social Nationalist party, etc.—to emulate the above-mentioned Arab Communist parties will tend to strip the Palestinian revolution of its essentially nationalist character, and create further dissension in its ranks.

3

The Palestinian Movement and the Arab States

Since 1948, when the Arab armies invaded Palestine in an attempt to destroy the newly proclaimed Israeli state, all Arab governments have been involved with Palestine. Some governments have been less concerned with the topic than others. Tunisia, for example, wanted to end the problem amicably in the early 1960s. Others have said they will fight for Palestine until Israel is militarily defeated and the Palestinian people are permitted to return to their own homes and form their own government.

By the end of 1948, 600,000 to 750,000 Palestinians had already fled Palestine and had settled as refugees in the neighboring Arab states. In May of 1967, the number of Palestinian refugees had reached 1,344,576; a large segment being third-generation Palestinians born outside of the state of Israel. Most of them were located in Jordan (722,687), Syria (144,390), Lebanon (160,723), and the Gaza Strip (316,776), which, until June 1967, was under Egyptian administration.[a]

The issue from the beginning has been primarily politics. There are approximately 1,600,000 Palestinian refugees now residing in Arab countries. Most live in the refugee camps of Jordan and Lebanon. Others live in camps established by the Syrian governments. Some live in luxury in Beirut and the Arabian Peninsula countries. Most, however, eke out a living performing menial labor, assisted by funds from the United Nations Relief and Works Agency for Palestine Refugees (UNRWA).

The mass uprooting and physical removal from their former homeland gave rise to bitterness, and resulted in the fragmentation of the Palestinian community and a complete breakdown of its social structure.

Those countries in which there were sizable Palestinian populations considered the Palestinian refugees to be political pawns. They constrained these displaced people to live in camps, giving them few amenities, and calling upon the world community to care for them since the refugees were the problem of those states who supported the creation of Israel. Lebanon and Jordan were the exceptions since their economies did

---

[a] Fred J. Khouri, *The Arab-Israeli Dilemma* (New York: Syracuse University Press, 1968), p. 378. These numbers refer to the Palestinians registered with the United Nations Relief and Works Agency (UNRWA) only. In Lebanon, for instance, the number of Palestinians is estimated at between 300,000 and 350,000. These numbers also do not refer to the entire Palestinian population.

41

not permit the absorption of all refugees into their social and business communities.

President Nasser of Egypt was the first to use the Palestinians as a paramilitary force. There was no need to use his own forces to harass the Israelis. Instead, he organized and trained units of Palestinians from Gaza and called them Fedayeen. He was to rue this decision since they were to encourage retaliation by Israel. Nevertheless, these Fedayeen had shown the way to counter Israeli charges that Palestinians were of no importance to the Arab world.

With the rising strength of the various Palestinian commando groups, the Arab states realized that their energies should be channeled lest they got out of hand and their own governmental processes disrupted. Thus, the PLO was formed in 1964 under Arab League sponsorship. It was only after the defeat of the Arab armies in June 1967 that the Palestinians came into their own. However, with the gain in strength by the groups, the Arab states began having difficulties with them. Syria, with a strong military, quickly clamped down on all guerrilla groups and maintained a tight reign on them. It created its own guerrilla group (Sa'iqa) and forced the other groups, Fatah, PFLP, and the military wing of the PLO, to adhere to its restrictions.

Iraq did the same, setting up its own group (ALF) and placing strict limitations on guerrilla activities inside Iraq proper. Egypt had no problem since Israel conveniently relieved the Egyptians of most of their Palestinian population by occupying Gaza and Sinai. Jordan and Lebanon had to bear the brunt of all Palestinian actions. Arrogance, flaunting of power, and frequent disruption of government business became the norm in these two countries. The problem was resolved finally in Jordan in 1971 when the guerrilla forces were chased into Syria, Lebanon, and across the Jordan River into Israel. Lebanon, however, because of its military weakness and religious segmentation, remains beleaguered, frequently under attack by Israeli forces and in a state of turmoil from guerrilla clashes with its armed forces. The main cause has been the ignoring of the accord carefully worked out by the two sides that was to list conditions for Palestinian action within Lebanon. (Detailed analyses of the interaction between the governments of Lebanon and Jordan and the Palestinian guerrilla organizations is included below.)

The guerrillas fare much better in the other Arab states. Libya, for example, has contributed heavily to the most radical groups, except the PFLP, which has a strong Christian leadership and Marxist ideas. The Persian Gulf states have a precarious relation with the guerrilla movement. Since they are being besieged by the Popular Front for the Liberation of the Arab Gulf on the one hand and asked to contribute to the PLO on the other, they are literally between the pan and the fire. If the Gulf states' regimes refuse to contribute, then the PLO groups will support the PFLOAG with arms, other materiel, and personnel.

The same could be said for Kuwait. Although the Kuwait government has, from the beginning, supported the guerrillas, permitting them to open offices, and to collect funds, its positive actions have been motivated partly by the fact that a large Palestinian community exists in Kuwait. This country had opened its door to the educated Palestinian refugees and provided them unlimited opportunities, in exchange for their economic and technical acumen. Although the Palestinians never stated it, the fact that this community is a potential fifth column against the Kuwaiti regime exists in many people's minds.

The Saudi government has no fear of threat from the Palestinians. By disbursing its oil revenues, the Saudis have bought the good graces of the PLO and Fatah. The government realized that the Palestinians are a useful tool to keep around in order to bring pressure upon those powers who are most influential in bringing peace to the area. By advocating the return of Jerusalem to the Arabs, and thus to the Palestinians, King Faisal served all Muslim people who then looked upon him as a savior.

Algeria has had close ties with the guerrillas since the Algerians were fighting for their independence. Palestinians supported the Algerian insurgents as best they could and were present at the Algerian guerrilla training camps. When independence was achieved, the Algerians permitted Palestinians access to the training camps and weapons. Currently, however, although continuing lip service and monetary assistance, the Algerian regime has tended to criticize the most overt terrorist acts committed by the guerrillas.

Tunisia has had little to do with the guerrillas. Morocco, however, taxed its people to provide assistance to the guerrillas. Notwithstanding the revolutionary nature of the movement, the regime paid tribute to the guerrillas. With the destruction of the Pan American plane in December 1974, in which several high-ranking Moroccans perished, support for the guerrillas has cooled perceptibly.

As was stated before, Jordan and Lebanon have had to bear the brunt of the Palestinian activities. As a result of guerrilla raids into Israel from sanctuaries located in these two countries, Israeli retaliations have been oppressive and devastating. Internal maneuverings by the guerrillas have brought further instability to Lebanon and Jordan. Today, Lebanon continues to exist under the threat of total disintegration caused in part by the presence of Palestinians, although Jordan has been able to free itself from a hostage position. The ensuing pages relate how these two countries reached their respective positions vis-à-vis the Palestinians.

Jordan

The kingdom of Jordan (previously, the princedom or amirate of Transjordan) owes its existence to the sagacity of its Hashemite monarchs and the nation-building role of its army. The Hashemite monarchs and the Jordanian army were both instrumental in overcoming the crises of the early formative stages of the state, and later on in weathering the repercussions of the first Arab-Israeli war of 1948 and the ensuing conflicts, both internal and external, over the future of the Arab inhabitants of Palestine.

The establishment of Transjordan was as much a by-product of efforts by Great Britain to implement the Sykes-Picot Agreement[b] as it was to placate its former Hashemite ally against Turkey during World War I.

Amir Abdullah, the second son of the Hashemite king of the Hijaz and a leader in the Arab revolt against Turkey, had reached Amman in March 1921. He had been entrusted by his father with the mission of raising an army from among the tribes with which to expel the French from Syria. Amir Faisal, a brother of Amir Abdullah, had been elected king of Syria in March 1920, and had been driven out of his kingdom by the French army during the course of the same year. Since lands east of the Jordan River fell, by virtue of the Sykes-Picot Agreement, under the British sphere of influence, Arab tribal incursions into the French-mandated territory of Syria would have had serious repercussions on British-French relations. The situation was resolved, however, by Winston Churchill who, in March 1921, was in Cairo, Egypt. Winston Churchill invited the Amir Abdullah to meet with him in Jerusalem, and on March 27, 1921, a joint agreement was concluded. The lands east of the Jordan would become the amirate of Transjordan with Amir Abdullah as its ruler. The new ruler agreed, in return, to prevent further incursions into Syria and Palestine.[1]

On March 22, 1946, the amirate of Transjordan was proclaimed the Hashemite kingdom of Jordan; and on 15 May 1948, the Arab Legion crossed the Jordan River to participate in the first Arab-Israeli war. In its aftermath, Jordan was to be subjected to the turbulent ramifications of what came to be known as the Palestinian Issue. The defeat of the Arab armies by Israel, the influx of a large number of Arab Palestinian refugees to Jordan, and the annexation of the West Bank into Jordan proper—with its demographic implications[c]—affected the political process of the king-

---

[b] The Sykes-Picot Agreement was concluded in secrecy by France and Great Britain in 1916. Basically, it stipulated that Lebanon and Syria would become French spheres of influence; Palestine, the lands east of the Jordan River, and Iraq would become British spheres of influence. Its publication in November 1917 by the Bolshevik government strained Anglo-Arab relations. The Arab nationalists had believed that Great Britain would help them create an Arab kingdom, comprising most of the Arab provinces of Turkey, in return for Arab support against Turkey.

[c] The population of Jordan trebled with the influx of refugees to Transjordan and the annexation of the West Bank of Palestine. With an original population of about 400,000 at the eve

dom and its army. Once more, the process of conciliation and force was employed by the Hashemite monarchs to achieve political control, which proved successful only to the extent that the Palestinians reacted negatively to the process of conciliation whenever "an alternative did seem to present itself,"[2] that is, Nasser and/or the Palestinian guerrillas.

Initially the British commander of the Arab Legion in the 1948 Arab-Israeli war was, as part of an Egyptian-inspired campaign, criticized by the Palestinian Arabs for having surrendered parts of Palestine (Lydda and Ramleh specifically) needlessly; and on 20 July 1951, King Abdullah was assassinated by a Palestinian for having met with Mrs. Golda Meir and having sought a permanent peace settlement with Israel. The process of Palestinian integration was, however, well underway and continued with major modification under the rule of King Hussein, King Abdullah's grandson.[d]

A survey of the Jordanian tribal families, especially the sedentary tribes along the eastern bank of the Jordan River, reveals strong kinship ties to the Arab inhabitants of Palestine.[3] Thus, divisions in the expanded Jordanian society were more political than social.

Politically, the process of integration had begun in the 1930s. The office of chief minister was, between 1933 and 1950, acquired almost exclusively by three native-born Palestinians: Tawfiq Abul-Huda, Samir al-Rifa'i, and Ibrahim Hashim. In the postannexation era, King Abdullah recruited loyal Palestinian cabinet ministers from among the rivals and enemies of Haj Amin al-Husayni, the ex-Mufti of Jerusalem, and president of the anti-Hashemite Higher Arab Committee. These then came from the Nashashibi family and the Nashashibi camp, and from such well-known Palestinian families as Tuqan, Jayyusi, Khayri, and Dajani. In all Jordanian cabinets, however, the Palestinians were outnumbered by the East Bank ministers; and a Palestinian Premier was generally appointed either to implement a policy the king knew would be unpopular with his Palestinian subjects, or in the aftermath of such an action to placate Palestinian nationalist resentment.[4]

The integration of the Palestinians into the Arab Legion was itself the result of a definite policy that was modified by geographic, financial, and social conditions. In anticipation of a likely role in the 1948 Arab-Israeli war, the legion was expanded. This expansion continued after the conclusion of the Israeli-Jordanian Armistice Agreement in April 1949, reflecting

of the Arab-Israeli war, it jumped to over 1,500,000. The 1,100,000 Palestinians were roughly divided between refugees and the actual inhabitants of the West Bank area. About 100,000 educated and trained Palestinians quickly filled the need for an expanding state, becoming Jordan's new middle and upper class. (For further information see: P.J. Vatikiotis, *Politics and the Military in Jordan: A Study of the Arab Legion 1921-1957* (New York: Frederick A. Praeger, 1967), pp. 8-13.)

[d] King Abdullah was succeeded by his son, Prince Talal, who was deposed in September 1952 for reasons of mental health.

by the direction it took the needs of the kingdom and the requirements of the legion.

The 1948 Arab-Israeli war and the conclusion of an armistice agreement transformed the mission of the legion from one dealing primarily with internal security matters to one encompassing defense of the territory. Moreover, the British evacuation of Palestine meant that the legion had to acquire the technical branches and skills hitherto provided by the British army in Palestine.

The expansion of the infantry and armored branches continued to reflect the traditional policy of recruitment of officers and men almost entirely from among the bedouin element. Their loyalty to the monarch and their natural warrior inclinations made them prime candidates for the expansion of the two core units of the legion. The expansion of the artillery and the development of engineer units and technical services (base and field work shops, a Base Technical Organization, and signal) reflected the adaptation of the legion to its mission requirements and the prevailing social conditions.

The officers and men of the artillery were mainly drawn from the townsmen and villagers of the East Bank, and the engineer units and the technical services' units saw a mixture of east and west bankers, with the west bankers predominating in the NCO and officers rank of some units. The fact that the engineer and technical services' units required skill, previous experience, and a higher degree of education made the west bankers and the urban east bankers natural recruits. Recruitment of east and west bankers was also based on the fact that the bedouin elements were not attracted to these units because of the manual work involved, and because these units were not considered to be fighting units.[5]

The development of a National Guard in the early 1950s originated with General Glubb, the British officer who became the head of the Arab Legion. The National Guard consisted of armed border villagers in the West Bank, trained, equipped, and commanded locally by legion NCOs, who would defend their village areas against border raids, or at least defend them until the legion could dispatch some reinforcements. Since the legion was hard-put to defend the borders with its meager resources, the National Guard would, from a practical point of view, relieve some of the legion units for other duties. Moreover, since most of the border villages were Palestinian, the National Guard, a force composed mainly of Palestinians, reinforced the process of integration.

The prospect of a large number of armed and trained Palestinians of dubious loyalty prompted the government to initially oppose its establishment; and some of the West Bank leaders, opposed to the annexation of the West Bank, also fought the establishment of a National Guard between 1949 and 1950 because of its integrationist thrust. At a later date, the status of the National Guard and legion control over it became the subject of a political tug-of-war between the Palestinian nationalists and the monarchy.

At this stage of the legion's expansion, British officers were in command positions at almost all levels because of general staff inexperience among Arab officers. Moreover, King Abdullah, suspicious of the ideologies of the extreme Right and Left, refused to appease those who opposed him.[6] Thus, those who were considered to be antiregime were excluded from participation in government and were banned from the legion.

Under King Hussein some of King Abdullah's policies were modified. The participation of suspected antiregime elements in the executive and legislative branches of the government was allowed, and officers with ideological inclinations were not excluded from the legion, or frozen in rank, until proof of inimical intentions were given.

In retrospect, whether one chooses to believe that King Hussein acted impulsively, reacted to events rather than having planned his moves, or was blessed with intuitive insights and providence, is immaterial. His actions were deliberate and showed political acumen and courage.[7]

In May 1953, political parties were allowed in Jordan. These included political parties with strong transnational inclinations toward Cairo and Damascus and ideologies inimical to the monarchy such as the Arab Nationalists, the National Socialists, the Ba'th, and the National Front—an electoral alliance of the Communist party and other leftists. In 1954 the Ministry of Defense went to a Palestinian in the Cabinet of Premier Fawzi al-Mulqi. In March 1956, the services of General Glubb and all British senior officers of the legion were terminated by the king in an effort to placate external criticism from Arab countries and to afford Jordanian officers senior command positions.[e] In October 1956, with the general elections over,[f] King Hussein asked Sulayman al-Nabulsi, the Palestinian leader of the National Socialists, to form a new Cabinet. The Nabulsi Cabinet was supported by the Ba'th and the National Front, yet excluded the pro-regime Constitutional Bloc.

The dismissal of the British officers and the formation of the Nabulsi

---

[e] General Glubb cites four reasons for his dismissal: (1) the intrigues of the King's Aide-de Camp, Ali Abu Nawar, whom he accuses of being a member of the Ba'th party; (2) an article in an English periodical that intimated Glubb and not the king was the real power in Jordan; (3) an attempt by the king to regain popularity and silence Syrian and Egyptian criticism in the wake of a fiasco generated by Jordan's expressed wishes to accede to the Baghdad Pact; and (4) the fact that the "King's mind and imagination had been genuinely fired by Arab Nationalism, precisely at the age when young men are most susceptible to the appeal of what appear to them to be idealistic causes!" (See: Sir John Bagot Glubb, *A Soldier with the Arabs* (New York: Harper and Brothers Publisher, 1957), p. 426.)

[f] In the general elections held in October 1956, the National Socialist, the Ba'th party, and the National Front showed a relatively strong following, especially in the urban centers. Out of a total of 40 seats, the National Socialists won 11, the Ba'th 2, and the National Front 3. The pro-regime Constitutional Bloc and Independents gained 8 and 9 seats, respectively. (See: Vatikiotis, *Politics and the Military in Jordan*, p. 125.)

government were quickly followed with the integration of the National Guard with the legion and the termination of the Anglo-Jordanian Treaty of 1948. Although the integration of the National Guard with the legion was in part an attempt by the Nabulsi government to infiltrate the army for political reasons,[8] it is also reasonable to assume that the king realized that integration would not jeopardize the army, and his agreement, therefore, must be viewed more as an attempt to disarm than to conciliate his political opponents. General Glubb seems to have shared the same opinion about the National Guard.

The program of political liberalization, however, was temporarily suspended when Sulayman al-Nabulsi and some of his Cabinet ministers were implicated in an abortive coup d'etat engineered by a small number of army officers. On April 10, 1957, King Hussein asked for the resignation of the Nabulsi Cabinet, and on April 25, all political parties were dissolved. In a sense the attemped coup d'etat discredited those involved to the degree that it may have actually contributed to the process of conciliation, and in the relative political calm of the early and middle sixties the process of conciliation resumed. By 1967 some of the 1957 antiregime politicians had been reappointed to Cabinet positions or had been allowed to run for Parliament. Moreover, the split between President Gamal Abdel Nasser and Haj Amin al-Husayni facilitated further the process of conciliation in Jordan. Members of the Husayni family were given Cabinet positions, and the settling of old feuds with the Hashemite monarch reduced the ranks of those Palestinian leaders who continued to view Nasser as an alternative to integration into a Jordanian society.[9]

The dissolution of the United Arab Republic (the union of Syria and Egypt) in September of 1961, Egypt's involvement in an internecine war in Yemen, and the successive bloody coups d'etat in Iraq did much to disillusion the remaining dissident West Bank politicians in their search for an alternative to Jordan. The politics surrounding the creation of the Palestine Liberation Organization (PLO) in 1964, and the selection of Ahmad ash-Shuqairy as its leader, contributed to the fragmentation of the Palestinian political elite and to the eventual emergence of a new elite, one that sought greater freedom of action within Jordan.

Jordan, for its part, suspecting that the PLO and the Palestine Liberation Army (PLA) were tools of Egyptian foreign policy, refused to comply with the decisions taken by the Arab leaders at the Second Arab Summit Conference in September 1964. It "limited and watched closely the PLO's activities within Jordan, refused to allow the PLA to recruit among the Palestinian units, and continued to draft Palestinians in the Jordanian army."[10] By 1968 the two sides had reached the breaking point. Palestinian militants were refusing to consider themselves Jordanians; they were first and foremost Palestinians. The Hussein government was adamant in refusing to recognize Palestinians in Jordan as other than Jordanian citizens. As the guerrilla movement gained momentum and strength following the 1967 war—the guerrilla forces began to flaunt their power, to parade with weapons, to establish their own form of government in the camps, and to overtly oppose United States attempts to conclude a peace settlement among the warring countries, which included Jordan—a clash became inevitable. The first one took place in November 1968, to be followed by three more and eventual annihilation of the guerrilla movement in Jordan.

Underlying Causes for the Clashes

A strong correlation exists between brightening prospects for a peaceful or political settlement of the Arab-Israeli conflict and the eruption of large-scale violence. The November 1968 clash ensued after a brief flury of activity at the United Nations enhanced prospects of a political settlement. The February 1970 clash erupted in the wake of United States diplomatic maneuvering, which resulted in the visit of Joseph Sisco, U.S. assistant secretary of state for Near East and South Asia Affairs, to some of the countries most directly concerned with and affected by the conflict. The June 1970 clash broke out as it became increasingly evident that Israel, Jordan, and the United Arab Republic were positively inclined toward an American Peace initiative; and the August to October 1970 clash came in the aftermath of acceptance by Jordan and the UAR of the "Rogers" or American Peace Plan. As far as the Jordanian regime was concerned, it can be concluded that:

1. Coexistance with the Palestinian guerrilla movement was deemed necessary as long as no viable alternative, political or military, to the Arab-Israeli conflict obtained. The guerrillas served a useful purpose. They kept the cease-fire line from becoming permanent boundaries, and they kindled international interest in a political settlement.

2. The use of force has always been part of the process of conciliation. The Jordanian monarchs resorted to the use of force when rival forces— political leaders, political parties, or tribal elements—refused to be swayed by the proffered political or financial rewards. At no time, however, were the goals of rival forces as irreconcilable with those of the monarchy as were Jordanian demands that the sovereignty of the state be upheld as paramount and the guerrilla insistence on freedom of action appear today, nor was there a rival force as powerful and widely based as the Palestinian guerrilla phenomenon. Thus force in the pre-June 1967 era was used infrequently. However, with the emergence of the guerrilla movement, force became increasingly indispensible to the process of conciliation. By the advent of the fourth Palestinian-Jordanian clash, force became paramount and conciliation was brought to a standstill.

3. The process of conciliation resumed after each of the first three clashes because drastic realignments in the Jordanian centers of power—

the king, the senior officers, and the civilian political leadership—did not occur. As long as King Hussein controlled his senior officers and chose to rule through the aegis of a government composed in the main of civilian political leaders, the process of conciliation could be resumed. Once confronted with a realignment of king and senior officers on the one hand, and the guerrillas on the other, the civilian political leadership could no longer function as an indispensible buffer in the process of conciliation. In the turbulent days preceding the fourth clash, it became evident that pressures, both internal and external, had forced a realignment of king and senior officers.

4. Regular armies, in general, and senior officers, in particular, consider the existence of irregular or guerrilla forces over which they have no command or control as a threat to their very own existence. In Jordan, that state of mind can be presumed to have been created with the emergence of the guerrilla groups. However, conditions that obtained in Jordan as a result of the June 1967 war—defeat of the Jordanian army, widespread sympathy for the guerrillas, and the absence of a viable alternative to continued warfare with Israel—prevented attitudinal antagonisms from being translated into behavioral aggression. It must be stated, too, that some of the senior officers, and a large percentage of the junior officers and the rank and file, were at first favorably disposed toward Fatah, the most moderate of the guerrilla groups. As long as Fatah was able to control the radical guerrilla groups and seemed willing to cooperate in the process of conciliation, an antiguerrilla attitude by some of the senior officers could not, by itself, force a realignment. Once clashes over respective goals began to be settled increasingly by a resort to force of arms, and once the army was called in as the final arbiter, the ability of both King Hussein to control the actions of his senior officers and Fatah to control the radical wing of the guerrilla movement was seriously undermined. The favorable predisposition of the army toward Fatah gave way to hostility as it did not extricate itself from the tempo of violence that pitted army elements against guerrillas belonging to the radical wing. A restive army—in part affected by the dismissal of some of its popular officers at the insistence of the guerrillas, and in part the result of the constant skirmishings that marked the months of June, July, and August 1970—and a monarch determined to resist guerrilla attempts to undermine his acceptance of a political settlement of the Arab-Israeli conflict, forged a realignment in the centers of power, which negated the role of and obviated the need for a civilian political buffer.

As far as the guerrilla movement is concerned, the following can be derived:

1. Willingness by the guerrillas to coexist was predicated on noninterference by the Jordanian regime in the affairs of the movement. Basic differences in the interpretation of what constituted noninterference, howev-

er, separated the moderate wing from the radical wing. The moderates, represented by Fatah, adopted a "live and let live" position, which derived from its nonideological orientation; that is, since the liberation of Palestine was the task of the Palestinians alone, and since the support of the Arab masses and their governments was auxiliary only, guerrilla interference in the affairs of Arab states and Arab state interference in guerrilla affairs was not warranted. The espousal of a Marxist-Leninist ideology by the radical wing led to a different interpretation; that is, to succeed in the liberation of Palestine, the Palestinian guerrilla movement should not detach itself from the Arab liberation movement, but should be part of it in its efforts to liberate the Arab masses from fascist or petit bourgeois governments. Thus, noninterference was one-sided: the guerrilla movement as a part of the Arab liberation movement could interfere in the affairs of Arab states, but these should be prevented from interfering in the affairs of the Palestinian Liberation movement.

2. Fatah, which by virtue of its noncommitment to the ideology of the radical wing was willing to use the process of conciliation to resolve outstanding differences with the Jordanian regime, refused to resort to the use of force in insuring compliance of the radical wing with the terms of agreements concluded with the regime. Fear that internecine warfare would weaken the movement prompted Fatah to seek "harmonization" as a means of achieving unity rather than the application of an Algerian solution to problems of Palestinian unity.

3. Harmonization as a means of achieving unity ultimately weakened Fatah and the entire movement with it. With force no longer a threat, the advantage passed to the radical wing. Harmonization accentuated the disunity of the movement, since the radical wing obstructed, without fear, all attempts to achieve a common approach to the military and political problems confronting the entire movement, unless such an approach conformed with its ideological orientation. The situation on the Israeli-Lebanese armistice line and the Israeli-Jordanian cease-fire line remained unresolved, and acceptance of the Peace Plan by Jordan and the UAR caught the guerrilla movement totally unprepared. Fatah, caught between its commitments to the government and its commitment to the principle of harmonization, was unable to choose. It, therefore, lost ground to the senior officers of the army and the radical wing, both of whom were actively seeking a final showdown.

Immediate Causes for the Clashes

An equally strong correlation exists between the actual outbreak of the four major clashes and the activities of the radical wing. The November 1968 clash was precipitated by Kataeb al-Nasr; that of February 1970, by the Popular Front for the Liberation of Palestine (PFLP); and those of June 1970 and August to October 1970, by the PFLP and the Democratic Front for the Liberation of Palestine (DPFLP), mainly. In all four cases, the radical wing was resisting by force of arms government attempts to enforce agreements, tacit or otherwise, concluded between it and Fatah, or the Fatah-dominated Central Committee of the PLO. In all but the first clash, it appears that the activities of the radical wing were deliberately calculated to provoke a major clash; and that in all of the last three clashes, the radical wing was motivated by both ideological considerations and fear lest a tacit alliance between Fatah and the regime would result in their suppression.

Strategy: Government and Guerrillas during the Clashes

The government strategy during the first three clashes was reactive and passive; that is, it depended on the strategy of the guerrillas for its own strategic reactions. It did not seek to take advantage of the situation to liquidate the guerrilla movement but, rather, sought to confine and isolate the conflagration. That it was reactive in nature is probably because of King Hussein who, it appears, preferred to use force judiciously to enhance the process of political conciliation so long as it appeared as a viable alternative to a final showdown. A close look at guerrilla strategy may also have, at first, convinced the king the price he would have to pay was too high. When peace based on Israeli withdrawal from the West Bank became a factor in the cost equation, and the process of political conciliation broke down, the army unfolded an imaginative and aggressive strategy, which, while expensive, proved partially successful. Based on a correct assessment of the strategy that the guerrillas would most likely adopt, the army developed a strategy that dictated to the guerrillas both the time and place in which its superior firepower and discipline would be brought to bear. It yielded control of the northern cities of Ramtha, Irbid, Mafraq, Zerqa, Ajloun, as-Salt, and Jerash to the guerrillas, choosing instead to beseige them and interdict their reinforcement and resupply capability, and it cleared Amman from guerrilla control with a combination of tanks, light armor, artillery, and mechanized infantry specifically tailored to minimize high army casualties. The fact that it was not totally successful was due to a faulty assessment of guerrilla determination and fighting capability, to the intervention of Syrian tanks directly in the fighting, and Arab League intervention to end the fighting before matters could be brought fully under army control.

Guerrilla strategy, on the other hand, was predicated during the first three clashes on a full realization of their weaknesses and strengths as well as those of the army. It was also predicated on a realizaton that the regime was seeking to control rather than liquidate their activities. Thus, a strategy was developed that would achieve the political objective—the lifting of restrictions and controls—by demonstrating that a military alternative was too expensive. It combined both positional and mobile warfare. Amman was to be fought for by the guerrillas and defended against an army assault by fortifying strategic positions in areas where guerrilla control was virtually undisputed, and by diversionary hit-and-run operations against government buildings and installations in the other areas of Amman and its suburbs. At all times, however, the population was to be used as shields.

Although fighting in the northern cities occurred infrequently and was light during the first three clashes, guerrilla strategy there was not based on positional warfare but rather on the absence of any front.

A faulty assessment of the army's loyalty appears to have influenced a radical change in guerrilla strategy during the fourth clash. Since it was believed that a large segment of the army would not obey orders to liquidate the guerrilla movement, positional and frontal warfare were judged to be the appropriate response. It was expected that a split army could not reduce a fortified Amman and breach the northern fronts simultaneously, and its attempts to take one position after the other would quickly bleed it of its strength. Had a split occurred in army ranks, it is conceivable that the guerrillas would have achieved a favorable stalemate that would have undermined Jordan's position in the peace negotiations.

Tactics: Government and Guerrillas during the Clashes

Government tactics during the first three clashes seemed to accentuate the reactive and passive nature of the government strategy. Roadblocks and checkpoints were used to cordon-off Amman from the rest of the country and guerrilla areas in Amman from the rest of the city. In a sense these were the two means used to isolate and confine the conflagration. Artillery and tank fire were used to silence guerrilla fire emanating from the Wahdat refugee camp and others on Jabal (Hill) al-Hussein, rather than as cover or suppressive fire in support of assault operations, and light armor and mechanized infantry were used inside the city to help repulse guerrilla sallies against government buildings, hotels, and embassies located on a hill not under guerrilla control. Yet judging from the effective tactics used during the fourth clash, which combined the use of artillery and tank fire with light armor and mechanized infantry in clearing the hilltops of Amman from guerrilla control, the impression is derived that the army had in fact been testing a number of tactical combinations all along to perfect those that proved most promising pursuant to the implementation of a strategy which envisaged street-to-street and house-to-house combat.

Guerrilla tactics were not basically altered during the course of four clashes. Possibly, the light armaments—rifles, AK-47s, light and heavy machine guns, RBGs, Katyusha rockets, and antitank mines—dictated the kind of tactic that would prove most successful in dealing with the superiority in fire power and discipline of the Jordanian army. Reinforced roadblocks, the approaches to which were protected by antitank mines and converging rifle and machinegun fire from elevated positions, formed the outer perimeter of the guerrilla enclave of Amman. The interior of the enclave was defended by a system of fortified machine gun emplacements at strategic locations capable of directing interlocking fire at an advancing enemy, and ambush squads and snipers were interspersed between one emplacement and the other.

In the northern urban centers, the proximity of guerrilla bases obviated the need for a defense in depth. Roadblocks were used to slow down an army advance, but in the absence of a solid front, the army preferred to challenge the guerrillas at long range with artillery and tank fire. Ambush operations and snipers were also put into effect on the approaches to these cities the mechanized infantry was most likely to take. With the invasion of Jordan by Syrian tanks and PLA units, guerrilla tactics were modified to conform to frontal warfare being waged by two regular armies.

Guerrilla Logistical and Reinforcement Capability

An awareness of the inherent weakness of a logistical and reinforcement capability that is dependent on one major supply road—from bases in Syria and Lebanon: the Beirut-Damascus-Dera'-Ramtha-Jerash-Amman (or Ramtha-Irbid) axis—and one minor supply road—from Basra up-river and then overland to Mafraq on the Mafraq-Irbid (or the Mafraq-Zerqa-Amman) axis—both of which could easily be interdicted, prompted the guerrilla movement to stockpile huge quantities of arms and ammunition in the urban centers and the bases in the Ajloun and Irbid areas. Huge stockpiles made each base self-sufficient, but in case of need, bases could become mutually reinforcing.

The creation of the refugee camp militias was also prompted by the above-mentioned awareness. In case of need, the militia could constitute the first line of defense until such times as the regulars took over—or they could constitute the huge manpower reserve upon which the guerrilla groups could draw for replacements. In either case, the need to evacuate guerrillas from hard-won bases in Lebanon, and others in Syria, would be obviated. In the first three clashes, and because of their short duration, the system was not tested. In the fourth, it broke down partially. Guerrillas in Lebanon and Syria evacuated their bases and rushed southward to Ramtha and Irbid, only to find that the road between Ramtha and Jerash and Jerash and Amman had been cut by the Jordanian army. It is not, however, clear whether these guerrillas were ordered to Jordan; and if so, it is equally unclear whether they were intended for the defense of the northern towns or whether they were supposed to proceed to Amman. In any case, their presence in Ramtha, Irbid, Jerash, or Amman could not have made a significant difference. What affected the guerrilla movement most during the fourth clash was the shortage of food and medical supplies. Guerrilla logistical planning either miscalculated or totally overlooked the need for such supplies.

Assessment at the Conclusion of the Strife

A correlation can be established between the demise of the moderates on both sides and the escalation of violence, and between violence and the rise to power of the radicals and the ultras. As far as King Hussein and Yasser Arafat were concerned, the following conclusions apply:

The agreements concluded at the end of the first three clashes were interpreted as setbacks for the Jordanian monarch. Yet in all three cases, promotion of the agreement was a definite attempt by King Hussein to enhance the prestige of Fatah and give it a chance to discipline the radical wing of the guerrilla movement. When Fatah failed to respond, pressure on the king mounted. At the conclusion of the February 1970 clash, the tribes rallied to the king in the belief that his position had been weakened. During the period between the June 1970 clash cease-fire and the conclusion of the settlement agreement on July 10, King Kussein came under pressure from his army visibly upset by the dismissal of his uncle, General Nasser Bin Jamil, and his cousin, General Zayd Bin Shaker, both of whom were extremely popular with the rank and file. The fact that King Hussein dismissed these two generals at the insistence of the PFLP created the distinct impression that the king had emerged from the June clash in an even weaker position than that in which he appeared to be at the end of the February clash.

Face, manhood, and valor are important considerations affecting the charisma of a leader in the Middle East, and especially with King Hussein's tribal subjects, the mainstay of his army and civilian support. The fact that King Hussein appeared to have capitulated shook the faith of his army in him. But the army was already shaken by the restraints that prevented them from meeting the guerrilla challenge. In some instances, troops were heard to complain loudly in the presence of the king that his actions had turned them into women; not being able to exercise their warrior profession had had the effect of robbing them of their manhood. By mid-August, the king, by his own admission, had almost lost control. The army was restive, and a definite threat of independent army action, bypassing his authority, existed. In a number of skirmishes during that period, there is evidence to suggest that certain army units were the instigators; and, by the ferocity of the engagement, a definite impression that these units were engaging in personal vendettas against the hated PFLP and DPFLP. There is also evidence to suggest that a number of antiguerrilla officers, at their personal initiative, fanned the fires of hatred.

Yasser Arafat was known personally to favor the monarchy and had striven to work within the system. His relationship with King Hussein had remained, throughout the four clashes, extremely cordial, and it was known that they both met frequently and generally referred to each other by their respective pseudonyms of Abu Abdallah (King Hussein) and Abu Ammar (Yasser Arafat). In a sense, it is possible to conclude that their friendship, and the good relationships that existed between Yasser Arafat and other Arab heads of state undermined Yasser Arafat's position. Moreover, with known high-ranking anti-Palestinians and antiguerrillas in the regime, the ability of Yasser Arafat to push for greater cooperation with the king was also seriously impaired. But the following tactical mistake, more than anything else, made Fatah a prisoner of its decisions.

Between June 1967 and the end of 1968, it is known that Yasser Arafat and Fatah objected strenuously to the decision that granted membership in the Palestine Liberation Organization to some of the radical guerrilla groups that were coming into existence. Yet Fatah chose not to make an issue out of it, although membership in the PLO gave these radical groups legitimacy and rendered the decision-making process of the PLO even more difficult. Having committed this initial mistake, Fatah compounded the situation by accepting the principle of "harmonization." In theory, the small radical groups were granted co-equal status, and they were quick on translating theory into practice. Fatah's paradoxical stand during the November 1968 clash and the April 16, 1970 demonstrations constitute the two other tactical mistakes. The November clash was instigated by Kataeb al-Nasr. Although Fatah cooperated with the government in settling the crisis, it chose publicly to come out on the side of the instigators. By so doing, it was placing itself in a position that would make it impossible for Fatah to disassociate itself in the future from the actions of other small radical groups. Publicly, and as far as the Palestinians were concerned, Fatah had absolved Kataeb al-Nasr and had indicted the government. Had Fatah chosen to indict Kataeb al-Nasr instead and forego the face-saving approach, it might have forewarned other radical groups that its support was not to be taken for granted. More important, by taking a firm stand during this minor incident, Fatah could have given its Palestinian and Arab supporters a lesson in objectivity.

The April 16 demonstration had a final and decisive effect on Fatah's leadership role and must be considered as, perhaps, the most serious mistake committed to date. Evidence suggests that agreement had been concluded between the government and the PASC to allow demonstrations, of a nonviolent nature, on April 14 and 15, but not on April 16, the day of Mr. Sisco's arrival in Amman. Although violence was committed during the demonstrations of April 14 and 15, and the government made no attempt to suppress the demonstrations, the PFLP, in violation of the tacit understanding, decided to hold further demonstrations on April 16. Guerrillas acting under PASC command were dispatched to the scene to stop the demonstration. For a moment it looked as if force of arms would be used against the PFLP, but once again Fatah yielded. By so doing, it had yielded its advantage to the radicals. They were now assured that Fatah would not use force or arms to enforce compliance with the terms of any agreement concluded between the moderates and the government, and, with that, the radical wing was freed of all constraints. As violence mounted, Fatah could neither extricate itself nor could it enforce discipline. The radicals within the guerrilla movement had gained the upper hand.

Driven into the small pockets of resistance, the guerrillas attempted to withstand the mopping-up exercises instigated by the Jordanian army. Unfortunately, their forces had been crushed during the battle for Amman. The Syrian forces refused to come to their aid, primarily because their main interest in entering the battle was to prevent the Jordanian army from chasing the guerrillas into Syria. The Ba'th regime did not want an organized and well-armed body of men crossing into Syria, creating an added burden for the state. Although opposing the Jordanians, the Syrians were, in reality, abetting the annihilation of Palestinian resistance.

One by one, the pockets around Jerash were eliminated. It was during this period in the summer of 1971 that Ali Abu Ayad fell. His death was to cause the creation of the Black September group, which has, in turn, brought death to many Jordanians. By August 1971, the guerrillas found themselves with only one base of operation—Lebanon.

Lebanon

As a result of the Arab-Israeli war in 1948, hundreds of thousands of Palestinians left their homes and settled in neighboring countries. Lebanon, as a member of the Arab community and a belligerent in the 1948 war, opened its frontiers to over 100,000 of these displaced persons.

Approximately half reside in 15 camps, established by the Lebanese government and maintained by the United Nations' agency. These camps are generally centered on the four principal cities of the country, with one exception. Near Tripoli, in the north, there are 2 camps, the Nahr al-Bared and the Badawi. The Beirut area contains 6 camps. Mar Elias lies within the Beirut city limits. The other 5 camps, situated in the vicinity of the capital, are Burj al-Barajneh, Shatila, Jisr al-Bacha, Dikwaneh, and Dbayeh. Near Saida (Sidon) are 3 more camps: Ain al-Hilweh, Mieh Mieh, and Nabatieh. Ain al-Hilweh is the largest camp located within Lebanon. Three Palestinian camps have been set up near Tyre. These are Rashidiya, Al-Buss, and Burj al-Shimali. The only camp isolated from the others on the littoral is located in Lebanon's inland Beka'a valley at Ba'albek—Wavell, which contains a very small population of around 4,000.

When the Palestinian refugees first fled to Lebanon, the majority of them suffered greatly from being uprooted from their homes. Their means of livelihood was limited to hand crafts, which were set up in the camps, and jobs found on the open labor market. Many were forced to exist on the doles supplied by the United Nations' welfare agency, for the economic situation in Lebanon in 1948 prevented the absorption of the refugees. Since the majority of the Palestinians were unskilled laborers and farmers, and since a scarcity of cultivable land and a paucity of jobs existed even for the Lebanese citizens, privation was common.

The fortunes of the refugees have improved over the years. With the expansion of the economic base of Lebanon, more jobs in industry and construction work were made available. Furthermore, the educational opportunities open to the Palestinians have afforded the younger generation the means to seek employment as white-collar workers, as businessmen and teachers; so that, today, Palestinians are to be found in all strata of the Lebanese business community.

The educated Palestinians had always had the opportunity to find more lucrative positions, not only in Lebanon but elsewhere throughout the world. Many left Lebanon and settled in the Persian Gulf region and the Arabian Peninsula, becoming successful businessmen or educators.

Full integration of the Palestinians into Lebanese society was an impossible task for the majority. Citizenship was awarded to some, but it was done according to certain precepts. The Lebanese government weighed carefully each application and fulfilled or denied the request on the basis of (1) whether the candidate was of Lebanese descent, and (2) in accordance with the policy of maintaining a six-to-five ratio in favor of the Christians.[g] Above all, there was a definite understanding among the Arab

---

[g] Since becoming an independent state, Lebanon has been governed according to an unwritten National Pact (1943) in which the president must be a Maronite Christian, the prime minister a Sunni Muslim, and so forth, until all religious denominations are represented in high-ranking government positions. This disposition of governmental powers was based on the 1932 census—none having been taken since—in which the Christians held a slight majority over the Muslims. To grant citizenship to all Palestinians, the majority of whom were Muslims, would have upset this balance and would have afforded the Muslim community a legitimate reason to demand changes on the basis of its being in the majority.

States and Palestinians not to dilute the Palestinian entity by integrating fully the refugees into the host societies, Jordan being the exception to this rule.

Acceptance of the Palestinians by Lebanese nationals was a further hinderance to their integration into Lebanese society. To begin with, the government considered the Palestinians to be a potential source of trouble inside the country. Egypt and Syria had used Palestinian elements in Lebanon for their own political aims in the past. This was the primary consideration for denying permission to the Palestine Liberation Army to operate within Lebanese territory, since these forces could be turned against the regime itself. Any Palestinian desiring to work with the PLA was free to leave the country but was not permitted reentrance.[h]

This consideration of the Palestinians as a potential subversive force was likewise held by many circles in the Lebanese society.[i] However, the Christian community was more adamant in its hostility than the Muslims. Desirous of maintaining the unique status of their country, separate from the Muslim masses that surrounded them, the Christians strove hard to create a "Switzerland," a country that would afford a safe haven to all. Their primary concern was commerce. Furthermore, although Lebanon's southern border abutted on Israel, Christians considered this boundary to be the most secure. They did not believe that Israel had expansionist designs on Lebanese territory. But if Israel did invade their country, the Christians firmly believed that the United States would come to their assistance, as they had in 1958, since the government had been a signatory of the Eisenhower Doctrine. What the Christians feared most from Israel was retaliation as was taking place in Jordan and Egypt. Therefore, in order to obviate the need by Israel to retaliate, the cause must be eliminated. The Palestinian guerrillas must be prevented from operating from Lebanon.

Similarly, the majority of the Muslim community shared with the Christians the belief that Lebanon must remain an independent country. They disagreed, however, on the theory of Israeli expansionism. For them, the intention of the Israelis was to invade and annex a part of Lebanon that would incorporate the Hasbani River, one of the three sources of the Jordan River. It was mandatory, therefore, for Lebanon to strengthen its position, not by looking toward the West and especially the United

---

[h] During the Khartoum Conference of August 1967, from which had come the unified course of action that the Arab countries should take, the Arab states had agreed that Lebanon should be exempt from assistance to the guerrillas because of her unique position in the Middle East. (See: John Cooley, "Beirut Shake-up Hints Guerrilla Ban," *Christian Science Monitor*, July 2, 1969, p. 2.)

[i] Professional jealousy, regardless of religious affiliation, also created adverse feelings toward the Palestinians. In 1966 it was hinted that the Intra Bank crash was handled ineptly by the Lebanese government, principally because the directors were Palestinians, although Christians.

States, which seemed to be the principal supporter of Israel, but by participating more fully in and aligning itself with the other Arab states. Thus, since President Nasser, who had abetted the Muslim community in the 1958 civil disturbances and was regarded with great esteem as the principal Arab leader, looked upon and furthered Palestinians as a potential force in the Arab world, the Muslims of Lebanon, then, should do likewise.[j]

Empathy toward the Palestinians by the Muslim Community was further enhanced by religious ties, since the majority of the refugees were Muslims, too. Nevertheless, a more definite and overt expression of support occurred only after the 1967 Arab-Israeli war had been concluded.

The June war, in essence, represented a new point of departure for the Palestinians. On the one hand, the constraints imposed by the Arab states, and within which the Palestinians operated, were destroyed by the Arab defeat. The Palestinian leadership, which had accepted these constraints and had placed its faith in the ability of the Arab armies to liberate Palestine, gave way to new leaders who were more familiar with the realities of the refugee camps and who rejected any form of Arab tutelage. The influx of new refugees from the Israeli-occupied West Bank and Gaza Strip on the other hand, served to reinforce the bond between the Palestinians in the refugee camps and the Palestinians living in occupied territory, and gave the Palestinian issue a new meaning.

With their newly acquired freedom and sense of purpose, the Palestinians now hoped to unfreeze the frontiers that had been defined following the first Arab-Israeli war.[11] Lebanon, because of its common borders with Israel and the presence of large numbers of Palestinian refugees on its soil, was not expected to play a vital role. The attempts to change the status quo resulted in serious fighting between the Palestinians and their host, the Lebanese government.

Underlying Causes for the Clashes

Although Lebanon remained uninvolved in the June war and, as such, did not experience the immediate effects of the war, it was, and continued to be, affected by the absence of a peaceful settlement and a resulting change in the attitude of the Lebanese people. The absence of peace and a transformed public opinion have, more than anything else, contributed to the increasing inability of the Lebanese governments to control its Pales-

---

[j] Insistance by the Muslim community was one of the determinants for adherence to the United Arab Command shortly before the war broke out in 1967, whereby the Arab states abutting on Israel would undertake united action in case of war. Lebanon, however, would not engage in an offensive war, but would defend herself if attacked.

tinian elements and keep Lebanon uninvolved in the undeclared war that has prevailed since the latter part of 1968.[k]

As long as a peaceful settlement seemed possible, the Palestinians constituted a source of embarrassment and were considered by many to be an obstacle to such a solution. As such, Lebanon's affirmation of continued adherence to the Armistice Agreement of March 23, 1949, and its acceptance of the Security Council Resolution [S/RES/242 (1967)] of November 1967 demonstrated the willingness of the Lebanese government to restore the situation to what it was before the 1967 war. These acts were also indicative of the difference between the aims and methods of the Lebanese government and that of the Palestinians. Israel's refusal, however, to be bound by the Israeli-Lebanese Armistice Agreement because of Lebanon's participation in the United Arab Command, and the insistence of the Israeli government on recognizing the 1967 cease-fire agreement, which it had concluded with the other members of the United Arab Command as equally applicable to Lebanon, gave rise in Lebanon to some serious misgivings about Israel's intentions. The Lebanese government interpreted this policy as evidence that Israel considered Lebanon to have been a belligerent, although Lebanon had not participated in the June 1967 war. Lebanese public opinion, on the other hand, saw the Israeli policy as a prelude to a possible invasion of Lebanese territory.[1] The Israeli raid on the International Airport of Beirut in the night of December 28, 1968, reinforced further the feeling in Lebanon that Israel had definite expansionist designs as far as Lebanese territory was concerned, and was no longer interested in Lebanon's continued existence.

The airport raid, in which 13 Lebanese civil airliners, valued at $43.8 million, were destroyed by Israeli commandos, represents a milestone in Israeli-Lebanese relations and a turning point in the attitude of the Leba-

---

[k] The Lebanese Army Commander, General Emile Bustani, refused to carry out the order of the prime minister, Rashid Karami, to attack Israel so as to relieve pressure on the Syrian Front. The implementation of such an order would have, in all probability, resulted in the destruction of the Lebanese army, and would have led to the occupation by Israel of some Lebanese territory. (See: "Lebanon Army Chief Rejected Order to Move Against Israel," *The New York Times*, June 21, 1967, p. 1.)

[1] The apprehension of the Lebanese is based on a statement made by General Moshe Dayan shortly after the application of the cease-fire in which he referred to the fact that Israel had acquired natural borders in the war with the exception of a natural border to the north. This was interpreted by the Lebanese to mean the Littani River. The Lebanese further allege the existence of a Zionist map that purports to show all, or parts, of Lebanon included in a Greater Israel. The Lebanese interior minister, Kamal Jumblat, states in an interview, that: "We have the impression that Israel wants to attack Lebanon. The design to annex certain territories in the south of our country, up to the Littani River which we have harnessed, has always existed. I will tell you more: I have seen certain geographic maps published in Israel which encompass all of Lebanon and parts of Syria, up to Alexandretta; in other words, the Syro-Canaan coast of antiquity." (See: B. Schwartz, "Israel Manages Lebanon," *Jeune Afrique*, no. 481 (March 24, 1970): 45.)

nese toward Israel. The raid was launched in retaliation[m] for an attack by two members of the PFLP on an El Al passenger plane two days earlier at the Athens airport. Lebanon was held responsible by Israel because the perpetrators had left Beirut for Athens on Lebanese travel documents provided to stateless persons, and had acted on orders of the PFLP, which operated in Lebanon with the apparent acquiescence of the Lebanese government. The Israeli raid was also a warning to the Lebanese government to curb the activities of the Palestinian guerrilla on its soil, and a warning to other Arab governments that continued support of the Palestinian guerrillas might, in the future, subject their own territories and property to Israeli retaliation.[12]

The Lebanese government categorically rejected any responsibility for the attack on the El Al plane in Athens, and the Security Council, which met to consider the matter at the request of Lebanon, agreed by unanimously condemning Israel on December 31, 1968.[n] The net result of the raid, however, was to move the Lebanese government and people closer to the Palestinians—the exact opposite effect of what the Israeli policy makers intended. The Government of Abdulla Yafi—a moderate on the Arab-Israeli conflict—fell, and was replaced with a government headed by Rashid Karami, who believed in military preparedness and stronger opposition to Israel.[13]

Lebanese public opinion, on the other hand, held that their country had been wrongly accused and that the raid was unjustifiable. Many saw it as an attempt by the Israeli government to further exacerbate the economic problems of Lebanon.

Poor in natural resources, Lebanon depends on the services it provides (banking, transit and free zone, tourism, etc.) and remittances from overseas Lebanese for its economic survival. The closing of Intra Bank, one of Lebanon's largest banks, on October 14, 1966, and the subsequent failure of a number of other Lebanese banks, shook the faith of the international community in the Lebanese banking system and in Lebanon as an international banking center, and precipitated a substantial flight of capital. The June 1967 war led to further increases in the flight of capital and seriously affected tourism for the remainder of that year. The Israeli

---

[m] The attack was also presumably launched in retaliation against the hijacking of an El Al passenger plane by three Palestinian guerrillas on July 23, 1968, while en route from Rome to Tel Aviv. The plane was forced to land in Algiers, Algeria, and was released with its male passengers and crew on August 31, 1968, in exchange for a number of Arab common law criminals held by Israel. (See: Richard A. Falk, "The Beirut Raid and the International Law of Retaliation," *American Journal of International Law* 63, no. 3 (July 1969): 417-18.)

[n] For the international legal implications of the Israeli raid, and the facts surrounding it, see: Falk, "Beirut Raid and the International Law," pp. 415-43. For an Israeli point of view, see: Yehuda Z. Blum, "The Beirut Raid and the International Double Standard," *American Journal of International Law* 64, no. 1 (January 1970): 73-105.

raid on the International Airport of Beirut ended whatever chances Lebanon had for a successful 1969 tourist season.

The business community was most affected by the economic situation. Composed mainly of Christians, and forming almost all of the Lebanese upper and middle classes, this community had, hitherto, refrained from supporting the Palestinians. Its continued viability rested now on greater economic cooperation with the Arab world, which, because of increased tensions in Arab-Israeli relations, meant support for the Palestinian guerrillas.

The failure of the Special Representative of the United Nations to secure agreement in accordance with the principles embodied in the Security Council resolution of November 22, 1967, had led to a hardening of both Israeli and Arab positions. Israeli mistrust of Arab willingness to abide by the terms of the Security Council Resolution, and Arab belief that Israel would not willingly withdraw from the occupied territories, led to a gradual escalation in military operations on both the Egyptian and Jordanian fronts, which ultimately culminated in the unilateral abrogation by Egypt on April 25, 1969 of the cease-fire agreement. With a peaceful settlement seemingly more remote than ever, the Palestinians emerged as potential allies of the Arab countries that had been involved in the June 1967 fighting.

Immediate Causes for the Clashes

Mindful of the increasing prestige and strength of the Palestinian guerrillas, and fearful of further Israeli raids, the Lebanese government attempted to impose, early in April 1969, stricter controls on the activities of the Palestinians in Lebanon, and especially those in the refugee camps. Armed clashes broke out throughout Lebanon between the Palestinians and Lebanese students, on the one hand, and Lebanese security forces on the other, resulting in 12 deaths and a large number of injured. On April 23, 1969, martial law was declared, and on April 24 Prime Minister Rashid Karami resigned amid widespread criticism.

On April 25 Fatah demanded freedom of movement and supply and the cancellation of the state of emergency and the lifting of martial law; and on April 29 the PLO expressed its determination to carry out operations from every country bordering on Israel. On May 6 President Charles Helou affirmed the support of Lebanon for the Palestinian struggle but insisted that the Palestinians must recognize Lebanese sovereignty and take into account the country's security. On May 31, however, in the wake of continuing clashes with the Palestinians, and after it became clear that the discussions between the Palestinians and the Lebanese authorities had reached an impasse, President Helou declared that he would not permit any actions that would enable the Israelis to retaliate.

In the absence of an agreement among the Lebanese political elements—no new government having been formed—and with the Lebanese-Palestinian negotiations at an impasse, the Palestinians had won a victory. Clearly, the Lebanese people had indicated their support for the Palestinians by refusing support measures that would lead to bloodshed. The Palestinians had defined their position and intentions, and it was now up to the Lebanese government to clarify its position and develop a working relationship with the Palestinian guerrillas.[o]

On August 11, 1969, Israeli planes bombed Palestinian guerrilla encampments in southern Lebanon—the first such raid after the Israeli air raid on the Beirut airport. Casualties included both Lebanese civilians and Palestinian guerrillas. In a speech broadcast by Israel, Mrs. Meir, the Israeli prime minister, stated that the raids were directed solely against the guerrillas. However, Lebanon must be held responsible for the actions taken by Palestinian guerrillas within its territory. Mrs. Meir commented further that if the Lebanese authorities refused to control the Palestinians, Israel would have to do it.[14]

Lebanon denied Israel's charges, insisting that the guerrillas in question were members of the Syrian-backed al-Sa'iqa sent by the Syrian government.[p] and complained to the Security Council. In the debates that followed at the United Nations, it became clear that Lebanon would not obtain the condemnation of Israel it sought because of the objections of the United States. Instead, the Security Council Resolution of August 25, 1969 condemned Israel's attack, and deplored the violations of the ceasefire. The resolution pleased neither party, but the remarks by Charles Yost, the United States chief representative, in which he placed blame for the raid on both Arabs and Israelis,[15] caused a wave of bitterness in Leba-

---

[o] Yasser Arafat had been asked to mediate the dispute between the Palestinians and the Lebanese government. At a conference held in Beirut on May 9, 1969, Yasser Arafat, in the company of Premier-designate Karami, was told by President Helou that the Palestinians would not be allowed to operate across Lebanon's borders without the approval of the Lebanese government. Yasser Arafat was told, however, that Lebanon would tolerate a guerrilla presence on its territory. But on June 24, President Helou demanded the withdrawal of all commandos from Lebanon. This request went unheeded. (See: John Wolf, "Shadow on Lebanon," *Current History* 58, no. 341 (January 1970): 20.)

[p] The claims made by the Lebanese government that the guerrillas in question were members of Sa'iqa who had infiltrated across Lebanese territory from Syria is, in all probability, true. The timing of the incident coincides with the power struggle in Syria between Generals Hafez Assad and Salah Jedid, the founder of Sa'iqa. General Jedid resigned his post as assistant secretary general of the Regional Ba'th party on May 29, 1969. It was feared too that Jedid would use the Sa'iqa to counter these Syrian army elements that had supported General Assad. As a result, a number of Sa'iqa leaders were arrested, and most of Sa'iqa was moved to the Lebanese border. (See: "The Commandos: Ideological Splits," *An-Nahar Arab Reports* (23 March 1970): 1.)

non. This remark was cited as another example of the one-sidedness of the foreign policy of the United States, and as the kind of support that would encourage further raids by Israel on Lebanese territory.

A statement made by Joseph Sisco, assistant secretary of state for Near Eastern and South Asian Affairs—which was distributed in Beirut by the embassy of the United States on October 12, 1969—added to Lebanese uneasiness about the intentions of the United States. In essence, the statement expressed the concern of the United States for Lebanon's sovereignty because of the violence being waged on its southern border. Above all he implied that his country would not remain impassive if Lebanon's integrity were threatened "from any source."[16]

A section of the Lebanese public interpreted Sisco's remarks as an attempt to "impose American tutelage."[17] Others criticized the statement for not differentiating between Israeli reprisals and the legitimate right of the Palestinians to their homeland; and for implying that Lebanon was threatened by countries other than Israel.[q] Others hailed the statement as a guarantee to Lebanon against Israel and support against the Palestinians. This group was to be shortly disillusioned when Israeli raids on Lebanese villages increased, and when the United States failed to support the Lebanese army during the major armed clash with the Palestinians, which erupted on October 22, 1969.

The two crises in Lebanon in 1969 between guerrilla and government forces were, in reality, one—the second being an extension of the first. Differences, however, are apparent and clearly differentiate the two. In the first clash, which took place in April-May, emphasis centered on control of the Palestinian refugee camps situated in Lebanon. The guerrillas needed the manpower of the camps, not only for recruits and supplies, but also to bring pressure to bear on the central government. During the second clash, which occurred in October-November, the guerrillas sought to establish bases in southern Lebanon from the sea to Deir Mimas, an area overlooking the industrial and agricultural region of northern Israel. Although the Lebanese authorities had tacitly ceded to the guerrillas their sovereignty over the Arkoub region, which is comprised of Mount Hermon and its environs, penetration into Israel from the Arkoub entailed two major hardships: the terrain was difficult to traverse and any guerrilla patrol was exposed to Israeli surveillance and gunfire.

The guerrilla personnel involved in the two clashes differed. During the first crisis, the radical element of the Palestine liberation movement, the PFLP (Popular Front for the Liberation of Palestine), was the principal instigator. Unwilling to wait until accommodations could be worked

[q] "Abdulla Sa'ade Explains the American Statement on Lebanon," *An-Nahar*, October 17, 1969, p. 2. Dr. Sa'ade was head of the Syrian Social Nationalist party, and strongly supported the Palestinian position in Lebanon.

out through negotiations with the Lebanese authorities, the PFLP used force in an attempt to isolate the government and to gain greater support from the Lebanese population. Those involved in the second clash were the more moderate elements, al-Fatah being the principal organization. They became affected when, in moving down from their bases around Mount Hermon toward the settled areas of south-central Lebanon, they ran up against the Lebanese army that had been positioned in this area to form a buffer between the guerrillas and the Israeli frontier.

Who initiated the clash was the third principal difference of the two crises. Whereas the guerrillas instigated the first clash by demonstrations, riots, and other tactics, the second incident was begun by the army whose leaders thought it best for the country to end the stalemate that existed after the conclusion of the first clash. The political and economic climate in Lebanon was deteriorating; the caretaker government was under constant pressure. A status quo could only bring further disorder in the long run.

Strategy and Tactics: Government and Guerrillas during the Clashes

The Lebanese authorities pursued three lines of attack against the guerrillas common to both crises. One, they attempted to retain control of the Palestinian refugee camps. In this, they were only partially successful. Since their forces had been forced to abandon posts inside the camps, they were unable to curtail such guerrilla activities as training and abetting the guerrillas by the inhabitants. However, the camps were cordoned and movement into and from the establishments was kept under rigid surveillance.

Two, the government attempted to rid the border area from the Mediterranean Sea to the Mount Herman area of guerrilla positions. This region was heavily populated and suffered loss of life and destruction of property caused by Israeli retalitory raids against guerrilla emplacements in the settled areas. Furthermore, the removal of the guerrillas from the border area was necessary to prevent a Lebanese-Israeli clash. The army knew it could not successfully stand up against Israeli forces and was afraid of being drawn into one by repeated Israeli incursions. During the first clash, the army was successful in neutralizing guerrilla forces in this region. However, when additional guerrilla units began moving into the towns, the army moved against them and began expelling all guerrillas toward the Mount Hermon area. This took place during the second clash.

The third strategical plan used by the Lebanese army was to gain control of the border region abutting on Syria in the Masnaa-Rashaya sector, thereby containing guerrilla units around Mount Hermon and gaining control of the principal supply routes used by the guerrillas to move men, equipment, and supplies into the Arkoub. In this way, they would be able to limit attacks on Israel from Lebanon. Again, this goal was pursued in both clashes.

Guerrilla strategy not only entailed gaining control of the camps, as was mentioned before, but it necessitated keeping their lines of communication open from Syria to southern Lebanon. The attack on Rashaya was a deliberate move to prevent closure of their main route to the Arkoub by Lebanese forces. In pursuance of their main goal, however, they failed to establish a string of bases across southern Lebanon. Only in the Arkoub were the guerrillas able to retain their dominant position.

It must be stressed that guerrilla strategy was formulated so some lines of communication remained open to the Beirut government. At no time did the guerrillas seek to completely rupture their relations with the Lebanese authorities.

The government blamed the guerrillas for the ills of the country. The government also attempted to create disunity among the Palestinian forces. This was done by appealing to Fatah, praising this organization for its moderate stance, while the radical elements were denigrated. During the first clash, too, the government felt strong enough at first to request that the guerrillas return to the Arkoub and, later, to demand that all guerrillas leave Lebanon. At the conclusion of the second clash, however, the government sought only accommodation with the guerrillas. Internal, as well as external, demands—political maneuvering, statements by religious leaders, President Nasser's efforts, and the general desire to prevent further bloodshed-persuaded the government authorities to resolve the crisis amicably.

Assessment at the Conclusion of the Strife

The Cairo Agreement was not a final settlement between the Lebanese authorities and the guerrillas. Instead, it was a written commitment by both parties to pursue a policy of accommodation in Lebanon. Specifics were to be worked out as the plan for cooperation was put into effect. Both sides had given ground to reach this accord—the government recognizing and giving specific rights to the guerrillas in Lebanon; the guerrillas agreeing to work within the context of Lebanese sovereignty and territorial integrity. Nevertheless, without the determination by both parties to make the agreement work, the situation in Lebanon would probably have deteriorated once more into open conflict between the guerrilla elements and the Beirut authorities.

Although the text of the agreement was to be kept secret for all times, a Beirut newspaper did publish what it claimed to be the true text. Since it was not denied by the government, and the paper was chastized for revealing what it should not have, it stands to reason that the following is the outcome of this very fruitful Cairo meeting:

Palestinian Existence. It was agreed to reorganize Palestinian existence in Lebanon on the following bases:

1. The right to work, residence, and free movement of Palestinians residing in Lebanon.
2. Formation of local committees of Palestinian residents in these camps through cooperation with the local authorities and within the framework of Lebanon's sovereignty.
3. Establishment of Palestine Armed Struggle Command (PASC) posts within the camps to cooperate with the local committes to insure good relations. These posts will be responsible for organizing and specifying the existence of arms in the camps within the framework of Lebanon's security and the Palestinian revolution's interest.
4. Palestinians residing in Lebanon shall be allowed to participate in the revolution through the PASC within the principles of Lebanon's sovereignty and safety.

Fedayeen (commando) Actions. It was agreed to facilitate fedayeen action by:

1. Facilitating movement by specifying passage and reconnaissance points along the border.
2. Insuring passage to the Al-Arqub (Arkoub) region.
3. PASC maintenance of the discipline of all members of the organizations so they will not interfere in Lebanese affairs.
4. Establishment of a joint disciplinary system between the PASC and the Lebanese army.
5. Cessation of propaganda campaigns by the two sides.
6. A census of armed struggle elements in Lebanon through the organization's leaders.
7. Appointment of PASC representatives to the Lebanese Army Staff to help solve all urgent matters.
8. Study of suitable concentration points along the border, which will be agreed on with the Lebanese army staff.
9. Regulation of the entry, exit, and movement of PASC elements.
10. Liquidation of Jayreen base.

11. Posts for medical treatment, evacuation, and supply for fedayeen action specified by the Lebanese army.

12. Release of detainees and confiscated arms.

13. Exercise of full powers and responsibilities in all Lebanese regions and under all circumstances by Lebanese civilian and military authorities.

14. The two delegations emphasize that the Palestinian armed struggle is in the interest of Lebanon as well as of the Palestinian revolution and all Arabs.

15. This agreement shall remain top secret and shall be accessible only to the leaders.[18]

It was signed then by al-Bustani and Arafat.

In reading the document, one is struck by how much the guerrillas were willing to concede to the Lebanese authorities. However, it is also quite apparent that Lebanese sovereignty was being impinged upon. Furthermore, some points were only outlined. This theme was recognized by Arafat when he said as he emerged from the session that contact between the guerrillas and Lebanese authorities would continue in Beirut.[19]

The major criticism of this document is the ambiguity found in many of the points. Without specifications and similar interpretations, each side could take a position it deemed to be correct.

But the Lebanese government expressed great satisfaction with the results of the efforts of their negotiating team. Karami, although claiming that the agreement was exactly what was desired, punctuated his remarks with the statement that the details were to be worked out in Beirut, thereby recognizing that the document had its imperfections.[20] These imperfections were to come to the fore as the two sides strove to implement the accords in the same spirit in which the document was negotiated—harmoniousness, calmness, and with respect for each others' position.

The Cairo Accord did legitimize the presence and activities of the Palestinian guerrillas on Lebanese soil and did guarantee the mutual noninterference of either party in the affairs of each other. The Palestinians, thus, were able to wrest control of the refugee camps away from the control of the Lebanese authorities. Coordination, on a partnership basis, in areas where Palestinian guerrilla activity could endanger the security of Lebanon, was now established to insure against future clashes.

There were initial minor incidents, which were to be expected. Certain guerrilla elements claimed the road between Masnaa and the Arkoub was now open to them. This claim was immediately challenged by an army captain who said he had received no orders supporting this.[21] Certain villagers in South Lebanon requested that Palestinian operations be transferred elsewhere than near their homes.[22] But, on the whole, harmony persisted between the two sides.

At the conclusion of hostilities between the Lebanese armed forces and the guerrillas in November 1969, the latter found themselves well-entrenched in Lebanon. The 15 Palestinian refugee camps were being controlled.[r] Much of the northern city of Tripoli, including the main fortifications, remained under their command or in the hands of sympathizers. North of Tripoli, the area was virtually abandoned by government troops. Both in Saida and Beirut were found quarters that had become armed encampments during the fighting.

On the Syrian border, a guerrilla force had penetrated deep into the south-central part of the country and had succeeded in linking up with other guerrilla contingents based in the Arkoub. This southern region of Lebanon had remained in guerrilla hands throughout the fighting. Known as "Fatahland," Lebanese authority had been virtually ceded to the guerrilla forces based there.

Amassed in Syria were approximately 3,000 additional commandos who would act as reinforcements if need be. This force was composed of members of the Palestinian Liberation Army and Sa'iqa. However, Sa'iqa and the PFLP had remained, for the most part, aloof from the second clash. Al-Fatah had been the guerrilla organization most involved with this second clash.

During the first clash, its leaders had tried to keep their followers from becoming embroiled in the altercations begun by the radical groups, PFLP and as-Sa'iqa. However, it was difficult not to be drawn into the fray since, to remain aloof from a struggle involving other Palestinian groups, dissension would be created among the Fatah ranks.

In the interim between the two clashes, Fatah had continued to pursue the same policy of trying to work through the Lebanese government in order to achieve freedom of movement for its members. Its intentions were outlined when a spokesman for the organization stated: "Fatah does not want to interfere in the affairs of the Arab states and asks from these states noninterference in their affairs."[20] It was impossible to refrain from fighting the Lebanese armed forces, though, when the latter attacked their positions in south-central Lebanon.

With all this pressure being brought to bear on the Lebanese armed forces, it would seem that the guerrillas held the upper hand during the

---

[r] The question of guerrilla control of the refugee camps was raised by Tekoah, Israeli ambassador to the United Nations in the General Assembly. He had proposed stopping all disbursements to the refugees since he was certain that the UNRWA supplies were going to feed the guerrillas, and the camps had been turned into training camps for future raiders of Israel. Although it is true that all police and gendarmerie posts inside and at the edge of the camps had been abandoned by the Lebanese authorities, the director of UNRWA stated that food allotments were not going to the guerrillas, and that the commandos did not interfere with the work routine of UNRWA officials. Furthermore, he knew of only six UNRWA buildings being used by the guerrillas. (See: Dana Adams Schmidt, "Commandos Rule 14 Refugee Camps," *The New York Times*, November 13, 1969, p. 1.)

negotiations in Cairo. Yet, they chose accommodation instead of further bloodshed and the possible disintegration of the Lebanese state. Their primary goal in Lebanon was to open up a second front against Isreal. Therefore, as Salah Khalaf of Fatah said before a group of students at the Arab University in Beirut, the guerrillas only intended to use Lebanon as a base from which to penetrate Upper Galillee. Above all, for them Lebanese sovereignty was sacrosanct.[24]

Throughout the ensuing months the details were painstakingly worked out. Lebanon granted to the guerrillas free reign in the Arkoub and permitted them the use of the Masnaa-Rashaya road for the importation of their supplies. (This, in reality, was a return to the status quo antebellum.) In exchange, guerrilla power in Lebanon except in "Fatahland" was whittled away. One of the first decrees to be published on the Palestinians was that guerrillas would not be permitted to wear their uniforms in Lebanese cities or villages.[25] This was followed immediately afterward by a proclamation that ordered the guerrillas to obtain a permit from the government for the purpose of holding a funeral procession.[26] This became necessary when machine guns were fired into the air by the guerrillas during a funeral procession. Armed men were thus forbidden to attend. More important, Lebanese security forces were ordered to escort the cortege.

The Lebanese government acted very wisely in appointing Kamal Jumblat as minister of interior at this time. A supporter of the guerrilla movement, yet an ardent Lebanese nationalist, he was chosen because he was friendly with the guerrillas and yet would not hesitate to tell them they were wrong. His presence during this difficult time helped both sides achieve as smooth a transition as possible. One example of his astute maneuverings is shown in the way the refugee camps returned to normal. Until mid-February 1970, the camps remained under the jurisdiction of 300 guerrillas who had been brought in to see to their administration during the fighting.[27] Jumblat was able to demilitarize these camps by establishing joint Palestinian-Lebanese control, in which the Palestinians would handle all Palestinian security problems and the Lebanese Gendarmerie would deal with ordinary and civil problems.[28]

Where the guerrillas and Lebanese ran afoul of the Cairo Agreement was in the border area adjoining Israel. Here the Lebanese government attempted to protect its people by circumventing the necessity for retaliatory raids by the Israelis. Through a series of decrees, guerrilla freedom of action was limited. On January 8, 1970, it was announced that the guerrillas would not be permitted to fire into Israel from Lebanese territory.[29] Instead, the commandos would first cross the border before initiating action. Jumblat also requested at this time that guerrilla camps be established no closer than 500 to 1,000 yards to villages inhabited by Lebanese citizens. He showed he meant what he said when on January 15 he closed commando offices in the villages of Hasbaya and Nabatiya.[30] To be fair to the guerrillas, the townspeople had demonstrated against the guerrillas and had set fire to the office in Hasbaya belonging to as-Sa'iqa. The closing down of the offices was intended to prevent any further disorders between the Palestinians and the Lebanese citizens. In this, Jumblat was following agreements worked out with the guerrillas in which the latter would refrain from entering inhabited areas.[31]

Commandos were also forbidden to carry firearms in the streets of cities and villages and were no longer permitted to train perspective recruits in the refugee camps.[32] The guerrillas were forbidden also to establish bases in south-central Lebanon.[33] Heavy weapons were no longer permitted in the Qura region of Lebanon.[34] All these restrictions were bound to cause protests and resentment from the guerrillas. But level heads prevailed. Yasser Arafat was determined to maintain as good relations as possible with the Lebanese government. As signator of the agreement, his honor and that of his organization and the PASC were at stake. Therefore, he sent statements supporting the actions taken by Lebanon. "There are no differences with Lebanon concerning the Cairo Agreement."[35] With his support, the implementation of the accord proceeded.

Even when, because of a misunderstanding, a Lebanese officer was killed and two of his men wounded, possible similar future incidents were prevented by the establishment of joint army-guerrilla patrols[36] and joint border control stations where the commandos would assist in organizing entry of guerrillas and their vehicles.[37] The army agreed at this time to halt the issuance of arms to Lebanese citizens who were opposed to the commandos.[38] Instead, national guard units would be formed, composed of men who lived in villages near the Israeli border. Weapons control would be achieved and the men would gain the satisfaction of believing they were training to defend their land against the true enemy, the Israelis.

Some opposition from the guerrilla groups was heard at the Palestinian Congress held in Cairo in May 1970. However, when the question of southern Lebanon was raised and how much the Lebanese authorities were restricting their movement and operations against Israel, the question was sent to a committee for further discussion from which it failed to reach the floor again.[39] Instead, watered-down statements of a general nature were enacted.

The fragility of the accord was proven very quickly when Israel launched a raid into Lebanon on May 11, 1970, which resulted in the destruction of private property and the deaths of private citizens.[40] This was followed two weeks later, May 22, by an Israeli bombardment during which 13 Lebanese lost their lives. Both attacks had been retaliatory, the second because of the destruction of a children's school bus by a rocket fired from Lebanon into Israel.

As a result of these raids, Lebanese refugees began streaming north into Beirut and other havens away from the fighting front. One paper in Beirut estimates that the number of people fleeing their homes in the south totalled 30,000.[41]

Government action was swift and to the point. It enacted a decree forbidding the firing of rockets from Lebanese territory.[42] Patrols were also forbidden, as were the carrying of firearms in cities and towns, a previous decree but one that had carried little weight.[43] Now these restrictive decrees were to be harshly enforced.

The minister of works, Pierre Gemayel, even proposed to the Parliament that all guerrilla action from Lebanon be stopped in an effort to prevent further retaliatory raids.[44] With the passage of time, however, and strong emotions subsiding, conditions began to return to normal. Members of the PLO were once again permitted to carry arms, but only with the foreknowledge of the Lebanese authorities.[45]

In this way, cooperation continued to prevail. Both the incoming president, Suleiman Franjieh, and his prime minister, Saeb Salam, expressed their support of the guerrillas as long as Lebanon's sovereignty was respected.[46] Yasser Arafat sent assurances to the president that the guerrillas would abide by the Cairo Agreement.[47] Because of the actions taken by King Hussein in Jordan against the guerrillas, the commandos realized the importance of this haven. Nevertheless, two factors tended to erode the guerrilla's position in Lebanon. First, internal dissension continues between the moderate and radical elements of the Palestinian movement. Independent acts by PFLP outside the working arrangements agreed to by Lebanese authorities and the guerrillas, such as rocket fire from Lebanese soil into Israel or the destruction of Tapline (oil) property near Saida, incurred the displeasure of the Lebanese government as well as the moderate guerrilla organizations. Internecine strife among the guerrilla organization, with the killing by Action Organization for the Liberation of Palestine personnel of a Fatah leader, also brought a sharp reprimand from Beirut authorities.[48] In November 1970, Yasser Arafat and other guerrilla leaders met in Beirut and attempted to organize the guerrilla elements so that incidents such as the above would not take place.[49] They agreed that the Palestine Liberation Organization would be the parent unit to handle all administrative guerrilla operations in Lebanon. Fund raising was now centralized; many offices were closed; and relations with the government would now be channeled through one central headquarters.

When the killing of the Fatah leader occurred in January 1971, Arafat moved swiftly to prevent similar incidents from taking place.[s] The suspects were apprehended by Fatah security forces and handed over to the Lebanese gendarmerie. The Action Organization for the Liberation of Palestine was disbanded, its offices closed, and its leader, Dr. Sartawi deported to Damascus.[50] As an added precaution, Arafat disarmed Fatah members. In this way, only authorized guerrilla personnel would be armed and would prevent indiscriminate or unauthorized shooting.

The second factor that weakened guerrilla positions in Lebanon was a loss of popular support. The peace overtures made by President Nasser and his successor, Anwar Sadat, created dissension between the guerrillas and the Muslim population in Lebanon. By adhering to the Egyptian Presidents' policy of a political settlement in the Middle East, some of the once ardent advocates of the Palestine liberation movement no longer abetted guerrilla activities from Lebanon (ergo, Ma'ruf Sa'd and his followers).

Nevertheless, the guerrillas were determined to retain their bases in Lebanon. Because of the situation in Jordan, Lebanon became even more important to the guerrillas. They did not want a similar crisis to erupt in Lebanon and for this reason, acted with caution and correctness within Lebanon. The Jordan crisis caused the number of raids into Israel to drop to 18 per month in 1970, possibly because of a reduction of guerrilla forces in Lebanon.[t] Yet, operations from Lebanon continued against Israel.

By 1972 southern Lebanon virtually was a battleground. Daily Israeli strikes and counter raids by the Palestinians were creating pandemonium among the Lebanese citizens who lived in this region. Furthermore, the country was in danger of a civil war erupting, with those who supported the Palestinians and those who believed the Palestinians to be albatrosses on opposing sides. In a showdown in June with the guerrillas, the Lebanese government came out the victor. Desirous of retaining bases in Lebanon and, more important, freedom from harrassment by the Lebanese army, the guerrillas agreed to curtail across-the-border operations and evacuate positions in the more settled areas of southern Lebanon. Furthermore, the guerrilla leadership was held responsible for any violation of this accord.[51]

---

[s] His moves had not come in time to prevent the murder of a prominent villager from Aitarun (a village located in the south), his father, and his pregnant wife by, allegedly, PFLP personnel. The man had been the head of the local militia organization Jumblat had established in the villages of the south to give the appearance of strengthening the defense of south Lebanon against the Israelis. These militia units had also helped the Lebanese security forces keep the guerrillas in line. (See: Eric Pace, "Multiple Murder Causes Lebanese Furor," *The New York Times*, November 19, 1970, p. 2.) Although the murders were never solved, suspicion continued to center on the guerrillas.

[t] The number of raids per month (February-September 1970) against Israel from Lebanon had averaged 52.

Unfortunately for the Lebanese, the guerrillas did not fulfill all terms of the accord. Following the killing of two Israeli soldiers in September 1972 by Palestinians, Israel sent punitive expedition into Lebanon's south, destroying much property and killing many citizens. This raid was, in fact, reprisal for the Munich killings. However, the incident that sparked the raid was the border incursion.

The Lebanese army began strengthening its position in southern Lebanon shortly after the Israeli invasion. Its forces systematically began evicting Palestinian guerrillas from the villages. The situation worsened when Syria, bent on defusing its Golan Heights border with Israel, terminated guerrilla operations from its territory and expelled guerrilla forces from the front areas.[52]

Many of those forced from the Golan Heights arrived on Lebanese territory seeking new bases of operations, thereby adding considerable numbers to those forces already opposing Lebanese authority. Inevitably clashes began on December 8, when Palestinians tried to reoccupy some of their former positions previously vacated.[53] The strife was to continue intermittently until the following May. At that time, after heavy fighting had taken place in Beirut and other population centers between the guerrillas and the Lebanese army, a compromise solution was reached whereby the guerrillas would refrain from storing heavy weapons in the refugee camps, as well as arresting Lebanese citizens and foreigners who were at odds with the movement.[54] Furthermore, the guerrillas would relinquish their virtual control of the camps and permit Lebanese authorities into the camp enclosures once more. In exchange, the commandos would be permitted to retain their bases in the Arkoub region of southern Lebanon and would receive the full cooperation of the Lebanese government.

These agreements, however, did not deter Palestinian guerrilla forces from launching raids into Israel, which resulted in severe reprisals from Israel. In fact, Israel blamed Lebanon for many of the terrorist operations staged against Israeli targets. Because of the devastation inflicted by Israeli forces, Lebanese civilians protested against the inaction of their government and demanded that something be done to end this aggression.

The Lebanese government finally reacted to these demands made by its citizenry. New defense weapons were purchased to protect the southern borders. However, the guerrillas, too, acquired defense weapons, primarily from the Syrian government, to protect their camps. This arms build-up augered further tension between the Palestinians and the Lebanese populace, tension that helped to create another serious clash in 1975.

Relations between the other Arab states and the Palestinian guerrillas is currently undergoing change. By seeking a peaceful solution to the Arab-Israeli crisis, the radical elements have lost much of their support. Relations have even improved between the Jordanian government and the

Palestinians, who once considered the Jordanian regime an anathema. By agreeing to relinquish all claims to any West Bank territory liberated from Israel, the Jordanians have set the stage for a reconciliation. The militant Palestinian elements continue to refuse to deal with King Hussein, but the moderates seem to have reconciled themselves to living with him.

The strong support envisioned by Egypt toward the Palestinian guerrillas seems to be sincere. Although they deplore terrorism, the Egyptians have, for the most part, steadfastly supported the Palestinian movement. Its sponsorship of United Nations recognition for the PLO is a strong indication of Egyptian policy. Yet, Syria seems to hold the key to the future of Palestinian affairs, as has been borne out in the ensuing warfare that engulfed Lebanon in 1975-76. The strong control held by the Damascus regime over certain Palestinian elements, and its hegemonic role over both Lebanon and Jordan, portends a future in which the Syrians will dominate any future Palestinian state.

4

The Rise of Terrorism

On July 23, 1968, the PFLP hijacked an El Al plane and flew it to Algeria. This act was the initiation of a policy designed to strike at Israeli targets wherever they may be located. Heretofore the guerrilla organizations had limited their actions against Arab lands or Israel proper. Now, however, an international aspect had been raised. Their acts could no longer be considered guerrilla warfare tactics. A new dimension had been added to the conflict: terrorism.

Table 4-1 contains a list of selected Palestinian terrorist acts. In each incident, the actor is designated wherever possible. Question marks do appear since the acts were never claimed by one group or cover names were used for the group. A third alternative is the case of an individual from a known group who acted on his own and the parent organization disclaimed responsibility. Under the heading "Target," this type of act, and sometimes the means, is also included. An asterisk by the date denotes whether bargaining took place. Other abbreviations necessary to read the table are as follows:

PFLP =	Popular Front for Liberation of Palestine
DPFLP =	Democratic Front for Liberation of Palestine
PSF =	Popular Struggle Front (also, known as PPSF)
BSO =	Black September Organization
Red Army =	Japan's United Red Army
PFLP-GC =	Popular Front for Liberation of Palestine-General Command
ANY =	Arab Nationalist Youth Organization for the Liberation of Palestine (also, known without the word "Arab")
OSOT =	Organization of Sons of Occupied Territory
OVZO =	Organization of Victims of Zionist Occupation
AOLP =	Arab Organization for the Liberation of Palestine
Other =	Individuals or small groups other than those listed above.

Table 4-1
Palestinian Terrorist Operations, 1968-74

Date	Actor	Target	Location	Objective
July 23, '68	PFLP (before PFLP-GC split)	El Al plane (Israel) [hijack]	Rome to Algeria	Acte de presence Prisoner release Intergroup rivalry
Dec. 26, '68	PFLP	El Al plane (Israel) [attack] (grenade, shooting)	Athens	Acte de presence Punishment Other
Feb. 18 '69	PFLP	El Al plane (Israel) [attack] (machine gunned)	Zurich	Punishment Other
May '69	PFLP	Tapline (U.S.) (bomb)	Golan	Punishment
July 18, '69	PFLP	2 Jewish-owned stores (Zionism) [attack] (fire, bomb)		Punishment Other
Aug. 25, '69	PFLP	ZIM (shipline, Israel) fire bombed [attack]	London	Punishment
Aug. 29, '69	PFLP and Latin American	TWA (U.S.) [hijack] (damaged plane)	Paris to Syria	Punishment
Sept. 8, '69	PFLP cubs	El Al office (Israel) [attack] (bomb)	Brussels	Punishment
" "	" "	Israeli Embassy [attack] (bomb)	Bonn	Acte de presence Punishment
" "	" "	Israeli Embassy [attack] (bomb)	The Hague	Acte de presence Punishment
Oct. '69	PFLP	Tapline/Zahrani (U.S.) [rockets]	Lebanon	Punishment
Nov. 27, '69	PSF	El Al office (Israel) [attack] (bomb)	Athens	Punishment Acte de presence
Feb. 10, '70	DPFLP (PFLP/AOLP (?)	El Al bus & lounge (Israel) [attack] (grenade)	Munich	Punishment Acte de presence
Feb. 20, '70	PFLPGC	Swiss Air (Switzerland, Israel) [bomb in air]	Zurich	Punishment Intergroup rivalry
Feb. 20, '70	PFLPGC	Austrian Air (Austria, Israel) [bomb in air]	Frankfurt	Punishment Intergroup rivalry(?)
Apr. 25, '70	Other	El Al office (Israel) [bomb]	Istanbul	Punishment
May 4, '70	Fateh	Israeli Embassy (shooting)	Paraguay	Punishment

Date	Group	Target [event]	Location	Objective(s)
June 7, '70	Other	U.S. (U.S. official kidnapped, one day)	Amman	Release of prisoners; Other
June 7, '70	Other	U.S. official (attempted kidnapping)	Amman	Release of prisoners; Other
June 9, '70	PFLP	Hotels (2) (hostages)	Amman	Defense of movement; Punishment
June 10, '70	Other	U.S. official (killed)	Amman	Release of prisoners
July 22, '70*	PSF (see Nov. 27, '69)	Olympic Air (Greece) [hijack]	Beirut to Cairo	Defense of movement; Punishment; Intergroup rivalry
Sept. 5, '70	PFLP, Latin American	PanAm (U.S.) [hijack]	Europe to Cairo	Defense of movement; Punishment; Release of prisoners
Sept. 5, '70*	PFLP	El Al-Israel (hijack)	Amsterdam to London	Defense of movement; Punishment; Intergroup rivalry
Sept. 5, '70	PFLP	TWA (U.S.) [hijack]	Frankfurt to Jordan	Release of prisoners; Defense of movement; Intergroup rivalry
Sept. 5, '70*	PFLP	Swiss-Air (Switzerland) [hijack]	Zurich to Jordan	Release of prisoners
Sept. 9, '70*	PFLP	BOAC (Britain)	Bahrain to Jordan	Release of prisoners
Apr. 2, '71	Other	Tapline (U.S., Jordan) [bomb]	Jordan	Punishment; Other
June 14, '71	PFLP	Liberian tanker (Israel/Iran & Saudi) [attack by rocket]	Red Sea (South Yemen)	Punishment; Other
Aug. 24, '71	Fateh (not claimed)	Alia plane (Jordan) [attack] (bomb)	Madrid	Punishment
Sept. 8, '71	Individual of Fateh	Alia plane (Jordan) [hijack]	to Libya	Punishment
Sept. 9 '71	Other	Tapline (U.S. Saudi Arabia, Jordan) [bomb]	Jordan	Punishment; Other
Sept. 15, '71	Other	Tapline (U.S., Saudi Arabia, Jordan) [bomb]	Jordan	Punishment; Other
Oct. 7, '71	Other	Alia Airline (Jordan) [bomb] no damage, before loaded	Beirut	Punishment
Oct. 24, '71	Other	Tapline (U.S., Jordan) [bomb]	Jordan	Punishment; Other

Date	Actor	Target	Location	Objective
Nov. 10, '71	Other	Intercontinental Hotel (Jordan, U.S.) [4 bombs]	Amman	Punishment
Nov. 28, '71	BSO	Wasfi Tal (Jordan [assassination]	Cairo	Punishment Acte de presence
Dec. 15, '71	BSO	Zaid ar-Rifai (Jordan [assassination attempt, just wounded] (machine gun)	London	Punishment
Dec. 16, '71	BSO Jordanian National Liberation Movement	Jordanian ambassador [bomb package] (3 wounded)	Geneva	Punishment
Feb. 8, '72	BSO	Gas pumping station (Netherlands, Israel) [sabotage]	Netherlands	Punishment
Feb. 8, '72	BSO	Elec. Gen. plant (Israel, Germany) [sabotage]	Hamburg	Punishment Other
Feb. 22, '72*	PFLP and OVZO	Lufthansa plane (Germany) [attack]	New Delhi to South Yemen	Punishment Financial gain
May 8, '72*	BSO	SABENA plane (Israeli target) [hijack]	Vienna to Tel Aviv	Release of prisoners Acte de presence
May 30, '72	PFLP and Red Army	Airport (Israel) [attack]	Tel Aviv	Punishment Acte de presence
Aug. 5, '72	BSO	Oil storage ctr. (Germany, Austria, Israel) [sabotage]	Trieste, Italy	Punishment
Aug. 16, '72	ANY(?), BSO(?)	El Al plane (Israel) [sabotage] (bomb)	Rome	Punishment Other
Sept. 5, '72*	BSO	Israeli Olympic team [kidnap]	Munich	Acte de presence Release of prisoners Defense of movement
Sept.-Nov. '72	BSO	Israeli officials and Jewish interests [letter bomb]	London, Rome and Geneva, Paris (worldwide)	Punishment
Oct. 6, '72*	Other (Palestinian students--individuals)	German Embassy (Germany)	Algiers	Release of prisoners

Date	Group	Target	Location	Motive
Oct. 29, '72*	(ANY)? (BSO)?	Lufthansa (Germany) [hikack]	Beirut to Yugoslavia to Libya	Release of prisoners
Dec. 20, '72	BSO(?)	U.S. Embassy [attack] (rockets)	Beirut	Punishment
Dec. 28, '72*	BSO/Ali Taha	Israeli Embassy [hostage]	Bangkok	Release of prisoner
Jan. 8, '73	BSO	Jewish Immigration agency (Zionism, Israel) [bombing]	Paris	Punishment / Other
Jan. 21, '73	Jordan Rep. Army-Punishment Forces	Tapline (Saudi Arabia, Jordan, U.S.)	Saudi Arabia	Punishment
Mar. 1, '72*	BSO	Saudi Embassy & U.S./Belgian officials [hostage]	Khartoum	Release of prisoners / Defense of movement / Punishment
Mar. 4, '73	BSO	Greek ship (Israeli tourism) [bomb]	Beirut	Other
April 9, '73	ANY	Israeli ambassador, El Al plane (bomb) [attack]	Cyprus	Punishment
Apr. 14, '73	Other	Tapline (U.S.) [bomb]	Lebanon	Punishment
Apr. 16, '73	Other	Tapline (U.S.) [bomb, exploded, no damage]	Lebanon	Punishment
May 2, '73	Other	U.S. ambassador's residence [rocketed]	Beirut	Punishment
July 19, '73*	OVZO (individual)	El Al office (Israel) [attack, fail]	Athens	Punishment
		Hotel [hostages]		Other (escape)
July 20, '73*	OSOT (Mt. Carmel Martyrs) and Red Army and Latin American (PFLP)? Haddad)?	Japan airlines (Japan) [hijack] (plane destroyed)	Netherlands to Dubai to Damascus to Libya	Punishment / Release of prisoners / Financial gains?
Aug. 5, '73	BSO(?) (7th Suicide Squad)	Airport passengers (Israeli tourism) (TWA to Tel Aviv) [attack]	Greece	Punishment / Other
Sept. 5, '73*	"Punishment" (Fateh and PFLP)	Saudi Embassy [hostage] Saudi Arabia officials [kidnap] (Target: Jordan, Saudi Arabia)	Paris Kuwait/Riyadh	Release of prisoners / Other (embarrassment of Arab govts.)
Sept. 11, '73	BSO(?)	Israel's Booth at Fair	W. Berlin	Punishment
Sept. 28, '73*	Eagles of Palestinian Revolution	Train from Russia [hostage] (Target: Israel, Austria)	Austria	Release of prisoners / Other / Acte de presence

Date	Actor	Target	Location	Objective
Nov. 25, '73*	(Sa'iqa) ANY	KLM (Holland, Israeli immigration) [hijack]	Beirut to Damascus to Cyprus to Libya, Malta to Dubay	Release of prisoners Punishment Defense of movement
Dec. 17, '73	Ghaffur's Group	(Italy, U.S. Peace Conference) PanAm plane & passengers [attack] (fire bomb, machine gun)	Rome	Punishment Defense of movement
		Lufthansa (Greece) [attack]	Rome to Athens to Kuwait	Release of prisoners Other (escape)
Jan. 1, '74	PFLP	British Zionist [attack] (shot)	London	Punishment
Jan. 25, '74	PFLP	Bank of Israel [bombing]	London	Punishment
Jan. 31, '74*	PFLP and Red Army and OSOT	Shell Refinery (Netherlands) [attack] (bomb)	Singapore	Punishment (escape)
		Ferry boat [hostage] (seajack)	Singapore	Other (safe passage)
Feb. 6, '74*	PFLP and Red Army and OSOT	Japan Embassy [hostages]	Kuwait	Other (provide Safe passage of Singapore group)
Feb. 3, '74*	Muslim International Guerrillas Ghaffur's Group	Greek freighter (target: Greece) [hostage] (seajack)	Pakistan	Release of prisoners Greek
Mar. 4, '74	ANY	British plane (target: Britain and U.S.) [hijack]	Beirut to Netherlands	Punishment
Apr. 11, '74	PFLP-GC	Israel	Israel	Punishment Other
May 15, '74*	DPFLP	Israel	Israel	Release of prisoners Acte de presence
June 13, '74	PFLP-GC	Israel	Israel	Punishment Acte de presence Other
June 24, '74*	Fateh	Israel	Israel	Acte de presence Release of prisoners Other

*Denotes bargaining

Column five denotes operational objects of the terrorists.

Defense of the movement is an important operational objective of Palestinian terrorism. Under this term we include initiatives undertaken to scuttle peace initiatives that may appear to threaten the realization of important Palestinian goals, and to support Palestinian unity and activism in opposition to Israel.

Some terrorist acts have clearly been undertaken as *actes de presence*, that is, for recognition. Although defense of the movement refers to the Palestinian movement as a whole, actes de presence are often employed to secure recognition for specific Palestinian groups, for example, Black September, PFLP, and the like. Another important aspect of the acte de presence is the advancement of worldwide recognition of the Palestinian cause.

Intergroup rivalry is a third operational objective. Several Palestinian groups have acted to demonstrate the efficacy of their own methods of supporting Palestinian goals or to gain greater prestige (and increased financial support, new material, or more recruits) relative to other groups.

Punishment—of persons, organizations, or countries—constitutes a fourth objective of Palestinian terrorism. The most obvious example of a punishment operation is the execution of Wasfi at-Tal, Jordanian prime minister, in 1971. Certain sabotage operations are also launched for punishment purposes.

A common objective of some of the more spectacular terrorist operations is *prisoner release*, that is, the freeing of jailed Palestinians, whether terrorists or other political prisoners.

Sixth, and finally, *financial gain* has occasionally served as the motive for undertaking a terrorist act. We are concerned in this case only with the financial gain as a direct result of the operation, not with financial rewards that may accrue later because Libyan or other financial backers are impressed with the efficacy of the group. To the extent this factor is a consideration in planning the operation, the objective for our purposes would be acte de presence.

It should be noted that the foregoing addresses *operational objectives*. It does not necessarily follow that the demands presented by terrorists in bargaining situations are identical with their objectives. Indeed, some obvious discrepancies arise. For example, safe passage out of the host country is a frequent demand of terrorists, but this is clearly not an operational objective within our meaning. Similarly, "defense of the movement," "acte de presence," "intergroup rivalry," and "punishment" are not generally used in the language of demand articulation by terrorists.

During the first two and a half years of Palestinian terrorism, the targets were primarily Israeli or Zionist. Occasionally, other countries were involved. Switzerland and Austria became targets when their national airlines were struck to deter tourism and immigration to Israel. Likewise, the United States became a target because of its total commitment to Israel.

The advent of the Jordanian-Palestinian conflict, however, in 1970 caused the Palestinian organizations to alter their policy. Jordan became an enemy and, as such, was subject to terrorist attacks. The debacle in Jordan in 1970-71 also spawned a new phenomenon—the guerrilla organizations whose specific raison d'etre was terrorism.

Terrorist Groups

The Black September Organization (BSO) was founded in 1971, and takes its name from the debacle that occurred in Jordan in September 1970, when Jordanian army units began suppressing the Palestinian guerrilla organizations. It is now recogized that the founder of this group was Abu Ali Iyad, a former Fatah leader who was killed during the fighting with Jordanian forces. The first operation of this organization was the assassination of the Jordanian prime minister in November 1971. Since then, the organization has been identified with acts of terrorism involving assassinations, letter bombings, hijackings, and sabotage. It has been identified with the operations carried out in Munich, Bangkok, Khartoum, Paris, and Athens. Because so much bloodshed has resulted from its mission, the BSO became an anathema to everyone, including the Arab countries and the Palestinian moderates.

The BSO has been closely identified with Fatah, principally because some of the men known to be a part of the latter have also been identified with the BSO. In reality, though, BSO acted independently of Fatah, and it was not until 1973 that Fatah leadership was able to control this terrorist organization. It is interesting to note, too, that since Fatah achieved supremacy, the BSO has not undertaken any terrorist missions.

The Arab Nationalist Youth Organization (ANYO) was founded sometime in 1971 by dissident members of the PFLP. Its known operations include the Lufthansa hijacking of October 29, 1972, the Cyprus incident of April 9, 1973, and the KLM hijacking of March 1974.

In 1975 very few operations were undertaken by the well-known terrorist groups or guerrilla organizations. The BSO is rarely mentioned anymore. The ANYO staged its last-known operation in March 1974. What has been happening is an attempt by Arafat to control these groups. Nevertheless, new names have been cropping up—the Organization of Victims of Zionist Occupation, the Palestinian Movement of Refusal, the Palestine Youths Organization, the Palestinian National Revolutionary Youth Group, the Palestinian Enlightenment Group, the Group for the

Return, the Revolutionary Group for the Martyrs of the Palestine Revolution, the October Group, and Nasir Group, to name some of them. What has been happening is that the actors for these operations belong to many groups, ranging from the PFLP to Fatah. Usually they belong to the militant segments of the organizations. They are dedicated to the Palestinian revolution and believe strongly in the use of force to resolve the Palestinian dilemma. In most cases they are prepared to become martyrs for the Palestinian cause.

In some instances Palestinian terrorists have been allied with members from other terrorists groups during a mission. The world was stunned when reading that three members of a Japanese radical group, the Red Army, had on May 30, 1972 attacked pasengers at the Tel Aviv airport, leaving some 26 dead before two of the terrorists were killed. The attack had been planned by the PFLP and was committed in the name of the Palestine revolution. Since then other operations have included personnel from other non-Palestinian radical groups. The hijacking of a Japan Airlines plane on July 20, 1973 involved both members of the Japanese Red Army and a Latin American who was the leader of the operation. Furthermore, the Singapore operation on January 31, 1974, and the follow-up operation in Kuwait a few days later when the Japanese embassy was seized by members of Palestinian groups as well as the Red Army group continued this policy.

The intentions of the Red Army terrorist organization was made clear when the organ of the PFLP, *Al-Hadaf*, published a letter that was a declaration of support for the Palestinian guerrillas from the Japanese Red Army.

We declare our readiness to meet our friends and launch armed struggles jointly with the Palestinians, to rout the Zionist enemy in offensive battles as soon as possible. . . . We urge the Palestinian and Arab strugglers, throughout the world, to launch the unified armed struggle against the common enemy. . . . We should choose the time, place, and target ourselves, because if we confine our struggle to a limited framework, this will be a factor assisting the enemy.[1]

A little over two months later the Singapore and Kuwait operations occurred. The world had been forewarned.

In 1972 the BSO continued the spectacular acts of terrorism it had begun the previous year, with the assassination of the Jordanian prime minister. Its members no longer concentrated solely on Jordanian personnel and interests. Israel became the principal target. Beginning in early February with the destruction of a gas pumping station in the Netherlands and an electric generator plant in Hamburg, West Germany,[a] the BSO struck

---

[a] Both targets were regarded as being closely linked to Israel since one supplied gas to Israel and the other, electrical generator equipment.

directly at the Israeli homeland with the hijacking of a plane to Tel Aviv on May 8. Although unsuccessful in its attempts to release prisoners being held in Israeli prisons, the BSO did prove that a guerrilla group was able to perform acts of international terrorism inside Israel itself. This fact was brought home to the Israelis even more when the PFLP, in conjunction with the Red Army of Japan, carried out a blood bath in the Tel Aviv airport on May 30. Three Japanese nationals killed 26 and wounded 60 persons in retaliation for the 2 BSO guerrillas who had been killed during the unsuccessful operation at Tel Aviv airport earlier in the month.[2]

BSO's most spectacular act of terrorism took place in Munich, West Germany, in September, when its members attempted to kidnap and hold as hostages the Israeli Olympic team. The reason given for this act was, again, the release of prisoners being held in Israel. The net result: 11 Israelis, 5 guerrillas, and 1 West German policeman killed and 3 terrorists captured. The outcome, although horrendous, could have had a happier ending, but for the intransigence of the Israeli government to refuse to negotiate, which was the BSO's primary motive in staging this act.

One other terrorist operation undertaken by the BSO in 1972, which was to gain worldwide attention, was launched in Bangkok, Thailand. The target was the Israeli embassy. This time, however, no casualties were incurred. Instead, the BSO came under strong criticism and much ridicule from other guerrilla groups for permitting such a fiasco. The guerrillas, after seizing the embassy, were persuaded by Thai officials and the Israeli captives to give themselves up in exchange for safe passage back to the Arab world.

In all the operations undertaken by the guerrillas, their objectives were, for the most part, clearly announced. Several pertained to the release of prisoners. During these operations, bargaining, or the attempt to bargain, was present. In others, the reason given or strongly implied was punishment. Wasfi Tal was assassinated because of his identification with the suppression of the guerrillas in 1970 and 1971. The Tel Aviv airport massacre was in response to the killing of other terrorists. The wave of letter bombs in Europe, which occurred in the last quarter of 1972, was meant to punish Israeli embassy personnel or those foreign nationals closely allied with the Zionist cause. Only one act in 1972 differed from the norm: the hijacking by PFLP members of a Lufthansa plane to South Yemen for purposes of acquiring ransom money. The others were punitive or sought the release of cohorts.

During 1973 terrorism continued unabated. Two events greatly shocked the world community: the assassination in Khartoum of two American and one Belgian diplomats, and the wanton firebombing and machine gun attack at the Rome airport of an American plane. Although the Arab world deplored these two incidents, it was able to respond with jubilation at the success of two guerrillas who succeeded in closing down the Austrian transit camp for Jews who were leaving the Soviet Union for Israel. There was a touch of the serio-comic—one a Japanese airlines carrier; the other, a KLM plane. In both cases, the passengers were carted all over the Mediterranean and the Arabian Peninsula before being permitted to leave the planes unharmed.

Whether it was due to improper planning, a more alert public, or a combination of both, many terrorist attempts failed during 1973. There was also a preoccupation with the underground warfare that had been escalating for the past two years. Spy killings by both Arabs and Israelis became commonplace and took place mainly in Europe. There is speculation that the assassination of Colonel Allon in Washington, D.C. was such an event in the "underground" war. Other casualties included, on the Israeli side, a member of the Brussels Israeli embassy staff, an agricultural counselor at the Israeli embassy in London, an Israeli "businessman" in Madrid, and an Israeli citizen in Nicosia, Cyprus. All were believed to be Israeli intelligence agents. The Palestinians, too, lost some key men to Israeli agents, including: Ghassan Kanafani, a spokesman and leader of the PFLP; Kamal Nassar, Kamal Adwan, and Abu Yussif in an Israeli commando raid in Beirut;[3] Muhammad al-Hamshari, the PLO representative in Paris; Dr. Kubaysi, an Iraqi university professor; and the unfortunate Ahmad Bouchiki, a Moroccan, who was gunned down by Israeli agents in Norway in a case of mistaken identity.[4]

Terrorism continued unabated in 1974. During the first quarter of the year, operations were staged against Zionist interests in London— the attempted assassination of a prominent Jewish merchant on January 1, and the bombing of the London branch of the Bank of Israel on January 25— and Singapore. The Singapore operation ended as a fiasco, with minimal damage being incurred at a Shell refinery and with deep involvement of the Kuwaiti and Japanese governments. The Shell refinery had been hit because of the strong support the Netherlands had given and continues to give to Israel. In this operation the Red Army once again participated, which in turn, embroiled the Japanese. Kuwait was brought into the scenario when terrorists seized the Japanese embassy in Kuwait, in order to extricate their co-conspirators who were attempting to extricate themselves from the debacle at Singapore.

Beginning on April 11, 1974, Palestinian guerrilla groups, using terrorist tactics, began to strike at the heart of Israel. Three members of the PFLP-GC staged a suicide raid at Qiryat Shemona and killed 18 Israelis before being killed.[5] The raid, itself, was aimed at undermining the position of the moderate Arab governments, which were heavily committed to the policy of a peaceful solution to the Middle East dilemma. The second terrorist raid into Israel took place on May 15, 1974 at the town of Maalot.[6] During this operation, staged by the DPFLP, 26 Israelis as well as the 3 guerrillas were to die. Judging from the confused reports reaching the outside world, the slaughter was needless since negotiations were involved (release of prisoners). The act itself was initiated to bring home to Dr. Kissinger and Mrs. Meir (who were at this time involved in peace negotiations) that Palestinians do exist and must not be discounted or overlooked in any peace settlement.

A third attack by guerrillas, this time members of al-Fatah, took place at Nahariyya. Total number of deaths: seven. It was a continuation of the "fight and talk" policy initiated earlier at Maalot and the Haifa refinery, which had also been bombed by al-Fatah commandos.[7] The entrance of al-Fatah as perpetrator of terrorist operations signalled a change of tactics on the part of its leadership. Heretofore, Fatah had denied participation in acts of violence, although it was common knowledge that BSO personnel were closely linked to al-Fatah. Now, fearing to be overshadowed by the radical groups, al-Fatah leadership realized that it, too, had to inaugurate a new policy that would deflate some of the adulation being given to the radical groups by their acts while, at the same time, to pursue a policy of attaining Palestinian recognition and territory through negotiations. It, therefore, adopted Hawatmeh's course of action of "fight and talk." Never let the Palestinian issue be placed on a back burner.

Israel retaliated by striking against the refugee camps in Lebanon, inflicting hundreds of casualties, both dead and wounded. Although the commando groups said their operations were initiated from inside Israel, the Israeli government held Lebanon responsible. The severity of the retaliation compelled the guerrilla leadership to notify the Lebanese government that it will assume responsibility for keeping terrorists from attacking Israel from Lebanon. Increased security by the Israelis, however, has netted several guerrilla teams crossing into Israel from Lebanon; and as part of their policy to deter guerrilla operations, the Israelis continuously have crossed over the Lebanese border to strike against alleged guerrilla encampments.

When tabulating the terrorist acts that have taken place since 1968, certain points should be stressed. The PFLP was responsible for most of the terrorist acts that took place between July 1968 and March 1974. The BSO was a close second. The terrorist groups also practiced certain types of acts as opposed to others. For instance, the PFLP concentrated mostly on attacks and hijackings while the BSO specialized in bombings and sabotage. Yet statistics show that of all the acts instigated by the guerrilla groups, most stressed bombings, with attacks coming in second and hijacking third. Israel, quite naturally was the recipient of most of these acts. However, Jordan was a close second. Fatah, because it basically refrained from acts of international terrorism, concentrated its attacks primarily against Israel and Jordan.

The objectives for these acts came also into focus. All groups stressed "punishment" as their primary reason for instigating an act, with "defense of the movement" and "acte de presence" following a close second and third. Hardly any were conducted for "financial gain."

Since a moratorium was set by Arafat for terrorist acts taking place outside Israel, the number of incidents decreased sharply. An occasional hijacking or hostage situation has taken place. But the rash of incidents, almost weekly, that had been occurring in 1972-73, is hopefully a thing of the past. Even before the moratorium went into effect, the number of incidents undertaken for punishment purposes decreased sharply. Instead, bargaining situations rose in 1973. Nevertheless, the radical splinter groups, extremists who refuse to adhere to a more moderate line, will, no doubt, continue to stage occasional spectacular operations, not so much as to achieve a specific purpose than to spotlight world attention on themselves. An important lesson learned from past terrorist acts is the will to die for the Palestinian movement. In the early operations, terrorists thought very much about saving their lives. With the arrival of members of the Red Army, a new concept was introduced—that of martyrdom. In dealing with certain governments, especially Israel, where bargaining is ruled out during terrorist incidents, martyrdom became a prime victory if one took the lives of as many of the enemy as possible before being killed. The terrorist has become an experienced person, able to perform well under stress, fully briefed in the terrorist tactics. Above all, the terrorist is determined to succeed in his mission, a determination that makes him a dangerous adversary. Since dissidents from many groups are banding together to perform terrorist acts in defiance of their leaders, their determination is combined with the feeling of hopelessness for a lost cause. This double characteristic thus portends future operations of a violent nature.

Although it has been the radical groups that have favored the use of terrorism, even al-Fatah has used extranormal acts of violence to better its position in the Arab community. Since first initiated in 1968, the number of terrorist acts has continued to mount. The reasons for doing so varies per group or act. Some operations are staged to tell the world that there is a Palestinian entity. Others are shown to be acts of vengeance. Still others are mounted to gain prestige within the Palestinian movement. The 1974 terrorist act committed at Kiryat Shemona by Ahmad Jabril's group, the PFLP-GC, were meant to disrupt peace negotiations.

Whatever the reason, as a weapon terrorism has been successful in keeping the Palestinian cause before the world community. Those members belonging to the "Rejection Front" have stated categorically that they will refuse to negotiate and that they will continue to use military means to resolve the Palestine issue.

If peace negotiations do not result in an acceptable and concrete solution to the Palestine question, there will be no alternative for the moderates but to revive their "fight and talk" tactics. Although it has been announced that al-Fatah will direct its operations solely inside Israel, it may change its scenario to the international arena. How long the moderates will be able to restrain the radicals is a debatable point. They will continue to put pressure on Israel by all means in order to force the issue and may be forced to use stronger tactics if negotiations drag on interminably. These tactics would probably include terrorism.

5 Conclusions and Outlook

Any attempt at assessment and projection must take into consideration the more than 50 years of Palestinian political and paramilitary experience. In terms of "lessons learned," the experience of these 50 years can, and should, be divided into three distinct phases:

1. The 1920-48 Arab Palestinian-Zionist Phase
2. The 1948-67 Arab States-Israel Phase
3. The 1967-73 Palestinian Guerrilla-Israel Phase

A reconstruction of the events in the 1920-48 phase would lead to the following conclusions:

1. The Palestinian leadership was fragmented between the founders of a number of political movements and the Higher Arab Committee of the Grand Mufti of Jerusalem, Haj Amin al-Husayni.

2. Attempts at achieving unity during the late thirties and the wartime years through internecine warfare, particularly between the leaders of the Istiqlal party and the Arab Palestine party, weakened the Palestinian effort to the point that the Arab League had to bypass them in deciding the future of Palestine;

3. All of the Palestinian political movements were similar in a number of respects. They were urban centered, with no mass following, but able to incite urban mob violence. They were founded by notables, almost all of whom were urban, and their membership was almost entirely composed of the land-owning or mercantile-urban classes. Furthermore, they tended to view Zionism and Jewish immigration as a political threat that should be dealt with mainly by peaceful means.[1] Thus, they tended to favor boycotts and strikes as a tool, and resorted to limited violence only when it served to reinforce their demands;

4. The bifurcation between politician and fighter, whether intended by the Higher Arab Committee or not, hamstrung the development of an effective guerrilla movement. The politicians, in their eagerness to maintain their control, were convinced that violence would preclude a solution.[2] They were thus willing to heed the advice of the Arab rulers in 1939, and accepted a truce with the Mandatory Authority without extracting a priori an agreement that could have insured the fulfillment of their objectives. The military or insurgent leadership was, on the other hand, willing to leave policy decisions to the political leadership. The net effect of this bi-

91

furcation was, however, that the Palestinians never mastered the political use of violence.

5. The absence of a platform that could be construed to represent the Palestinian program for action most probably hurt the development of a genuine mass movement and gave the effort its negative image. If a platform did exist, it was based on the principle of noncooperation with the Mandatory Authority; and whatever appeal was made to the masses, especially in the rural areas, was made in terms of defending the "land and religion against the infidel."[3]

The Palestinian issue is transformed, during the 1948-67 phase, and assumes a broader Arab character. The basicity of the issue—Palestinian Arabs versus Zionism—is diffused and becomes the Arab-Israeli conflict. The Palestinian Arabs lose their freedom of action and become actors instead of directors or, more specifically, wards of the Arab states; and the Arab countries adopt the Palestinian issue as their own, although they do not assume specific responsibility for it.

This phase is important because of three major developments:

1. The creation by Egypt of the Gaza-based Fedayeen
2. The establishment of the Palestinian Liberation Movement (PLO)
3. The emergence of young "radicals" among the Palestinians

In 1955 the Egyptian authorities and, specifically, Egyptian Army intelligence, began to organize commando groups. Recruited from among the Palestinian refugees of the Gaza Strip, the commandos were both a tactical weapon (to hit specific Israeli targets), and a source of intelligence. It is not as yet clear what prompted the creation of these commando units, but the timing coincides with a number of events in the area.

A reported difference of opinion between President Nasser and the Grand Mufti, who moved his headquarters subsequently to Beirut, may have at first impelled the Egyptian authorities to organize the Palestinians into Egyptian army affiliated commando units as a means of curbing the influence of Haj Amin al-Husayni. Israel's role in what is now known as the Levon Affair may have, on the other hand, hardened the Egyptian position and led it to use the commandos as a means of retaliation. Finally, the impending Egyptian-Czech arms deal and fears of a preemptive attack by Israel, may have moved the Egyptians to use the commandos for their intelligence-gathering requirements. The use of the Fedayeen by Egypt, however, proved to be one of the major catalysts of the 1956 Suez war.

Since the Fedayeen were acting under Egyptian orders, their activities cannot be considered as a Palestinian attempt to pursue their struggle with Israel. Rather, the importance of the Fedayeen is to be found in the fact that some Palestinian guerrilla leaders who emerged shortly after the June 1967 war came from the ranks of these commando units.

Nasser emerged from the 1956 war as the undisputed leader of the Arab world and hero of the Arab masses. It was natural, therefore, for the Palestinians to turn to him for a solution to their problem and accept his leadership. Nasser, in turn, could not ignore their presence or refuse to heed their plea for action. Although his suggestion for an Arab recognition of a Palestinian entity was matched by similar declarations of interest on the part of some of the other Arab states, it also aroused their suspicion; for the Arab world was entering what has been called "the Arab Cold War."

For the Palestinians, the discussions that surrounded the recognition of a Palestinian entity by the Arab states represented a positive although hesitant first step. The fact that a Palestinian organization came to exist finally in 1964 is, to a large degree, due to the efforts of Ahmad ash-Shuqairy.

Shuqairy did not belong to the pre-1948 Palestinian leadership, nor to the many factions of the 1950s and early 1960s. He had served as head of the Saudi Arabia delegation to the United Nations from 1958 until September 1963, when he was dismissed from his post for refusing to present to the United Nations a Saudi Arabian complaint against Egypt. He was immediately appointed by the political committee of the Arab League to represent the interests of the Palestinian refugees at the United Nations. Shuqairy was thus eminently qualified "to head the type of organization which the Arab states were inclined to establish—an organization set up in their own image with the functions of a quasi-government, and possessing a parliament and its own army."[4] In other words, the leadership of the PLO was removed from the realities of the refugee camps, and gradually became a captive of Egypt, involving therefore, the Palestinians in the Arab Cold War.

The fact that the Palestinians would not be given any degree of independence by the Arab states, and the Palestinian leaders would not seek to challenge Arab control, was recognized as far back as 1956 by a small group of Palestinians then considered to be radicals or militants. This group of radicals created the Movement for the Liberation of Palestine or Fatah. The leadership of Fatah disapproved of the close links between the PLO and the Arab League, which involved the Palestinians in inter-Arab rivalries, and was critical of the "go-slow" policy enunciated by Nasser. Recognizing the general weakness of the Arab world, they disagreed with those who believed that "time was on the side of the Arabs," and insisted that "time was on the side of the Israelis."[5] They also postulated that guerrilla warfare, and the Palestine Liberation Army (PLA) or the Arab armies, would defeat Israel, because it would reduce considerably Israel's technological advantage.

The fact that Fatah itself is a child of inter-Arab rivalries is important only if related to the future course of the Palestinian guerrilla movement. In all probability, Fatah would have been relegated to "obscurity had not the Syrian Government, strongly opposed to Egyptian domination of Arab policy, decided to sponsor its own 'liberation' organization. This sponsorship lasted until the June war of 1967."[6] Viewed as an alternative to the PLO of Shuqairy in outlook and approach, Fatah emerged, therefore, as the only post-1967 faction to which most Palestinians could rally in their efforts to regain Palestine.

In the 1967-73 phase, the emergence of Fatah as the single most powerful guerrilla group is of utmost importance for the following reasons:

1. Its membership is placed between 80 and 90 percent of the total strength of the guerrilla movement.
2. Its leadership is closer to the realities of the refugee camps.
3. It has successfully avoided involvement in inter-Arab rivalries, and has successfully bridged the ideological gap between Saudi Arabia on the one hand, and countries like Iraq, Syria, Algeria, Libya, and Egypt (under Nasser) on the other.
4. It has sought unity of action through consensus, and has successfully avoided the pitfalls of imposing its will over other members of the PLO by force of arms, which could have resulted in internecine warfare.
5. It has merged the political and military decision-making process into a single body within Fatah, thereby avoiding the dangers of bifurcation, although it has not been able to impose this fusion on other guerrilla groups who are members of the PLO, except in such limited cases as the Palestinian Armed Struggle Command (PASC) and the Unified Command of Palestine Resistance (UCPR).

In short, Fatah seems to have made every effort to avoid the mistakes committed during the first two phases, and remains today, through its control of the PLO, the only *interlocuteur valable* for the Palestinian guerrilla movement.

More recently, and as a result of the decision of the Rabat Summit and the General Assembly of the United Nations, the PLO has been recognized as the only *interlocuteur valable* for all Palestinians. Since Fatah still controls the decision-making process within the PLO, essentially the decisions of Fatah will determine the future of the Palestinians in the foreseeable few years. The most pressing decisions that Fatah will face are:

1. How to deal with the "Rejection Front" and other dissidents
2. The formation of a government in exile
3. Continued warfare and negotiations with Israel

4. The secular state and other formulas

5. The prerequisites of a viable Palestinian state

The Rejection Front and Other Dissidents

The Palestinians can be divided into three main categories: the majority who favor a peaceful settlement; a minority that basically is in favor of a peaceful settlement but rejects it so as to give the Palestinians an out in case peace hopes are dashed; and a minority that rejects a peaceful settlement regardless. The Palestinian guerrillas accurately reflect this division. The majority—Fatah, Sa'iqa, and the DPFLP—have come out in favor of a negotiated settlement; the PFLP and the ALF constitute the "rejection front;" and the PFLP-GC and other small elements fall somewhere in between. This is not to say that disagreement does not exist among the leadership of each of these guerrilla groups. These disagreements do exist, will be exacerbated, and will surface more clearly once the terms of a negotiated settlement are clarified; and it can be expected that some shifts may take place as to the ultimate alignment of these groups and the factions within each. But the fact remains that a negotiated settlement will be the approach favored by a majority so long as Fatah and Sa'iqa continue to support it.

In dealing with the Rejection Front, Fatah will, in all probability be guided by basic policies. First, Fatah can be expected to avoid any course of action that will either lead to, or give the impression of, internecine warfare. As it has done in the past, when major disagreements among the guerrilla groups threatened to split their ranks irrevocably, Fatah will postpone a decision of an ultimate course of action, and will rely on mediation and pressure by Arab Governments as a means of reaching consensus. In the case of the Rejection Front, this is certainly applicable since the PFLP has not broken with the PLO completely, but has withdrawn from the Executive Committee only. Second, Fatah, will avoid any course of action likely to involve the PLO in inter-Arab rivalries. Since the Rejection Front is supported, directly or indirectly, by Iraq, the Peoples Republic of South Yemen (although this support appears to be cooling), and Libya, and since Iraq and Libya do constitute the Arab Rejection Front that opposes Presidents Sadat and Assad, attempts by Fatah to deal with the Palestinian Rejection Front by direct means will involve Fatah and the PLO in inter-Arab rivalries. Fatah and Sa'iqa, however, are likely to deal very ruthlessly with dissidents from within their own ranks. Ahmad Ghaffur (ex-BSO/RASD) was assassinated once he left Libya, and

Abu Nidal (Sabri al-Banna) ex-Fatah member, has been sentenced to death by Fatah and will probably be eliminated the moment he leaves Iraqi territory. Fatah has acted decisively, and is guided in doing so by its overriding concern with the maintainance of discipline.

The Formation of a Government in Exile

The necessity to create a Palestinian government in exile has been raised, discussed, and rejected or postponed several times in the past few years. Although Fatah seemed amenable to the idea, it has taken no action to push for the creation of such a government for the following reasons: First, the creation of such a government was likely to split the Palestinian guerrilla movement over the question of representation and the number of portfolios, as was almost the case with representation in the PLO and the Executive Committee; second, there is basic disagreement as to what purpose a government in exile would serve that was not now being served by the PLO's Executive Committee, as well as the repercussions that might ensue. It was argued, and widely held, that the creation of a government in exile would detract from the dynamism of the Palestinian guerrilla movement by forcing it to act in the static ways that governments act, that such a government would be a harking back to the days and style of Ahmad ash-Shuqairy, and that it might lead to political entrenchment associated with the leadership of the 1930s and 1940s.

More recently, and since the October 1973 war, the matter has become more urgent in light of the Rabat decision and recognition granted the PLO by the General Assembly of the United Nations. Saudi Arabia and Egypt, backed by Syrian agreement, seem to be pressuring Fatah to create a government in exile. Although Fatah has indicated its willingness to go along, several obstacles have to be overcome before such a government can be created. In all probability, Fatah will insist on PFLP representation (1) to achieve a unified PLO front, and (2) to avoid embroiling the PLO in inter-Arab rivalries. To that effect, it has sought the support of Iraq and has achieved some success. More important, the PLO will have come to grips with the terms of a negotiated settlement that will be acceptable to the membership of the PLO, and the overwhelming majority of the Arab states having the USSR and the United States as the necessary go-between. Fatah will have to come to grips with the kind of state, its structures and ideology, that it proposes to establish if negotiations result in the creation of a Palestinian territorial entity (see below: the "Secular State"). Finally, a general understanding must be reached with Jordan that will, to the satisfaction of both parties, give body to the Rabat decision and Jordan's acquiescence.

Continued Warfare and Negotiations with Israel

The question facing Fatah is not whether to continue warfare if Israel refuses to deal with the PLO, or whether to suspend warfare once a negotiated settlement has been achieved, but what to do while Israel deals with the issue of direct negotiations with the PLO, and what policy to adopt once these negotiations take place (presuming Israel show a willingness to deal directly with the PLO or a PLO designated representative body).

A decision appears to have been taken by the PLO (all factions to include the PFLP) concerning the course of action it should adopt while Israel deals with the issue of direct negotiations with the PLO or a designated corporate negotiator. On the one hand, the PLO has, from all indications, decided to suspend all its operations in the international arena with the exception of Israel. Given increasing European support or neutrality, the apparent willingness of the United States to act as a "honest broker," and the support of all of the Communist world and the Third World, it can be concluded that the PLO leadership feels it has made its case, and that continued terrorist activities in the international area (except Israel) will prove to be counterproductive. Hence the decision by the PLO to try the hijackers of a British Airways airplane (Dubai-Tunis, November 21, 1974).

The decision, on the other hand, to limit operations to Israel or Israeli held territory, with all of the guerrilla groups in the PLO participating in guerrilla raids, appears to be the result of several factors. First, the PLO leadership is convinced that Israel is less likely to negotiate with the PLO if pressure is not maintained. However, and probably more important the PLO leadership is determined to avoid the mistakes of the 1930s when the leadership then agreed to a truce without extracting, a priori, an agreement that could have insured the fulfillment of their obectives. Second, support and recognition by most members of the international community and by the General Assembly of the United Nations has legitimized the Palestinian struggle, and, therefore, action of a military or terroristic nature against Israel is both legitimate and serves to keep the attention and the pressure of the international community focused on Israeli refusal to abide by United Nations resolutions concerning Palestine and the Palestinians, and Israeli refusal to negotiate with the internationally recognized representatives of the Palestinian people, namely, the PLO. Third, willingness to engage in military and terrorist acts by those who have indicated their acceptance of the principle of a negotiated settlement enhances their stature within the PLO and undermines the position of their detractors who accuse them of *istislam* (defeatism) and a willingness to sell out. Fourth, limiting military and terrorist attacks to Israel serves a psychological purpose. It is a constant source of hope for those Palestinians under Israeli occupation, a constant reminder to potential Palestinian elites who might be tempted with Israeli and/or Jordanian encouragement to present themselves as viable alternatives to the PLO, and a way of demonstrating to the Israelis that there is no alternative to the PLO and that a negotiated settlment cannot be concluded without the PLO.

The Secular State and Other Formulas

The Palestinians have come a long way from Ahmad ash-Shuqairy's "throwing the Jews into the sea," to the secular state proposed by Yasser Arafat at the November 1974 meeting of the General Assembly of the United Nations. The Israelis, too, have come a long way from Golda Meir's statement that there were no such thing as Palestinians, to the more recent recognition by Premier Rabin and Foreign Minister Allon of the existence of a Palestinian problem. With this in mind, the secular state formula should be looked at a bit more seriously, and from two points of view, namely, the external meaning and the internal meaning.

The never fully elaborated concept of a secular state was, in a sense, forced on Yasser Arafat by the PFLP and DPFLP who, recognizing the strength of Fatah and the support it received in the Arab world, were anxious to pin down the exact relationship among the various guerrilla groups in the postsettlement Palestinian entity. To be more exact, they were concerned with their participation and role in the decison-making process in a future Palestinian entity. The setbacks and bitter experience of the PFLP in securing greater representation and greater role in the Executive Committee of the PLO is a reflection of that concern. Initially, Yasser Arafat would only state that "the socio-political composition of the state would reflect the ideological orientation of the liberators."[7] At a later date, Fatah modified this position, without basic alteration. It stated that:

A democratic and progressive Palestine, however, rejects by elimination a theocratic, a feudalist, and aristocratic, and an authoritarian or a racist-chauvinistic form of government. It will be a country that does not allow oppression or exploitation of any group or people by any other group of individuals; a state that provides equal opportunities for its people in work, worship, education, political decision-making, cultural and artistic expression.[8]

Thus, it is clear that the secular platform enunciated by Fatah rejected by omission the Marxist-Leninist approach of the PFLP, and, therefore, attempted to achieve a consensus. Also, it must be remembered that the PLO was trying to correct the negativistic approach of the 1930s by putting forth a platform that could be the basis for a positive dialogue once negotiations started.

Since the October war, the PLO has publicly endorsed the secular state formula, although privately, and especially Fatah, it has indicated its willingness to consider a territorial formula that would be based on a compromise between the 1948 partition plan and an entity based on the West Bank and the Gaza Strip. These contradictory formulas are best explained if one considers the following: (1) that Fatah is hamstrung by the absence of the PFLP from the Executive Committee of the PLO, and is, therefore, unwilling to endorse the second formula publicly until the PFLP, through the concerted efforts of all of the Arab states, is forced to rejoir the Executive Committee and accept the second formula; (2) that Fatah is awaiting the outcome of the quadripartite conference (Sadat, Assad, Arafat, and Hussein), which would determine the positions of each at Geneva, if and when the conference is reconvened, and the representational formulas that would be adopted (whether the PLO would be part of the Jordanian delegation, or whether it would be its own negotiator); and (3) by the unwillingness of Israel to deal with the PLO. Israeli unwillingness, whether real or temporary, forces the PLO and/or Fatah to adopt an extreme prenegotiation stance.

The Prerequisites of a Viable Palestinian State

The Palestinians have, for some time since the October war, been discussing the prerequisites of a viable Palestinian state. Although the political aspects were studiously avoided in such discussions, there is nonetheless some consensus as to the leadership, structure, and relationship with the Arab world.

It is widely held that, in a transitional period (estimated to be two to five years) the proportional representation of the various guerrilla groups and independents represented in the PLO and its Executive Committee will be reflected in the decision-making process of the new state. However, because of Israeli objection to the PLO, a facade of "independents" is not excluded. But these "independents" will be nominated by the various guerrilla groups and members of the PLO and will, proportionately, reflect the present distribution of seats in the PLO and the Executive Committee. Also, it is widely held that the Palestinian National Congress will be transformed into a constituent assembly that would draw-up a constitution which would most likely create an elected National Assembly or Parliament (unicameral), an independent Judicial Branch, and a strong but elected Executive Branch composed of a president and his Cabinet.

In this transitional phase, it is expected that the various guerrilla groups would transform themselves into political movements or parties, representing the ideologies they espouse, and will contest the election on this basis. Thus, the system will also be based on the multiplicities of political parties or movements. However, it is also widely held that the system will change after the national elections to reflect the orientation of the winner, and it is predicted that the system that will evolve will be similar to that of Algeria: a single party system in control of the state, ruling directly or indirectly through a special relationship between single party and state mechanism yet to be defined. If this process actually takes place, it is expected that Fatah would take over the new state, and that its ideological orientation will be closer to Egypt's under Sadat, than either that of Syria or Algeria.

Then, too, the Palestinian guerrilla movement is concerned with the economic-manpower prerequisites of the new state, and has addressed itself to this problem. Economically, and because of the absence of mineral resources in either the West Bank or the Gaza Strip, the PLO has come to the conclusion that the new state will need an infusion of between $5 and $16 billion to take care of initial problems, such as housing, settlement, agricultural development, and the bureaucracy. Only Saudi Arabia appears capable of meeting this kind of need.

More important, and posing a dilemma, is the manpower needs. A viable new state needs to in-gather all of its manpower resources, especially its intellectual and commercial elites, and its white- and blue-collar workers. The problem for the new state is not limited to the approach it has to take to entice this necessary manpower from the Gulf areas, Lebanon, Libya, and the United States (to mention a few), but whether and at what rate it should entice them back since they hold lucrative jobs that could be important sources of revenue, providing some of that revenue reaches the new state in the form of remittances to parents and relatives.

Syria, though, will dictate terms for a viable Palestinian state. Its strong position taken in Lebanon during the recent crisis is an indication of its hold over the Palestinians. With Syria as the guarantor, the PLO could accept an Israeli-Jordanian settlement that would restore the West Bank and Gaza to Jordan, with the understanding that elections in the West Bank and Gaza soon after would determine the political structure of the kingdom. In any case the impasse over mutual recognition between Israel and the PLO would be sidestepped, and Israel's insistence that Jordan be the negotiator would have been met. The future of the West Bank and Gaza—whether it remains united with Jordan or becomes a separate Palestinian entity—should not pose a problem, since in any case it would be linked to the Syrian-Jordanian-Lebanese entente; and, as such, both Jordan and Syrian would in fact take the responsibility for the behavior of that Palestinian entity and underwrite its existence. In concrete terms, such an approach would mean that this new entity would not need the trappings of a new state, that is, an army, nor would it necessarily mean that Palestinians now living in Lebanon, Jordan, Syria, and other Arab states would be forced to return en masse to the West Bank and Gaza creating a *lebensraum* problem. Economically, this Palestinian entity would be more viable as a result of its links to the Jordanian-Lebanese-Syrian entente and would benefit from common trade, tourism, and services.

Notes

Notes

Chapter 1
Introduction

1. Geoffrey Furlonge, *Palestine Is My Country: The Story of Musa Alami* (London: John Murray, 1969), p 80.

2. George E. Kirk, *A Short History of the Middle East* (New York: Frederick A. Praeger, 1955), p. 179.

3. Abdul Majid Abbass, "Palestine (1933-1939)," in *Challenge and Response in Internal Conflict,* eds. D.M. Condit and Bert H. Cooper, Jr. (Washington, D.C.: The American University, Center for Research in Social Systems, March 1967), ch. 3, p. 66.

4. Hisham Sharabi, *Palestine and Israel: The Lethal Dilemma* (New York: Pegasus, 1969), p. 186.

5. Furlonge, *Palestine Is My Country,* p. 90.

6. Ibid.

7. Sharabi, *Palestine and Israel,* p. 186.

8. Norman and Hellen Bentwich, *Mandate Memoirs 1918-1948: From the Balfour Declaration to the Establishment of Israel* (New York: Schoken Books, 1956), p. 53.

9. See: Furlonge, *Palestine Is My Country,* p. 107; and Abbass, "Palestine (1933-1939)," p. 67.

10. Sharabi, *Palestine and Israel,* p. 187.

11. Abbass, "Palestine (1933-1939)," p. 68.

12. Sharabi, *Palestine and Israel,* p. 189.

13. Christopher Sykes, *Crossroads to Israel* (Cleveland: The World Publishing Company, 1965), pp. 265-66.

14. Ibid., pp. 204-380.

15. Barbara Wilson, *Palestinian Guerrilla Movements* (Washington, D.C.: The American University, Center for Research in Social Systems, 1969), p. 15.

16. Ibid.

17. Wilson, *Palestinian Guerrilla Movements,* pp. 22-23.

18. Ibid., p. 24.

19. Ibid., p. 25.

20. Ibid., p. 26.

21. John Cooley, *Green March, Black September: The Story of the Palestinian Arabs* (London: Frank Cass, 1973), pp. 90-91.

22. Ibid., pp. 136-37.

23. Wilson, *Palestinian Guerrilla Movements*, p. 36.

24. Ibid., pp. 100-101.

25. *The Arab World* (Beirut), August 27, 1971, pp. 11-12.

26. Ibid., July 14, 1971, p. 4.

27. Ibid., September 15, 1971, p. 11.

28. Ibid., June 7, 1972, pp. 11-12.

29. Ibid., October 16, 1972, pp. 5-6.

30. Ibid.

31. John Cooley, "Guerrillas Envision Role in Peace Talks," *Christian Science Monitor*, October 26, 1973, p. 3.

Chapter 2
The Palestinian Revolutionary Movement

1. Michael Hudson, "The Palestinian Arab Resistance Movement: Its Significance in the Middle East Crisis," *The Middle East Journal* 23, no. 3 (Summer 1969): 298.

2. Hisham Sharabi, *Palestine Guerrillas: Their Credibility and Effectiveness* (Washington, D.C.: Georgetown University, 1970), p. 45.

3. Hudson, "The Palestinian Arab Resistance Movement," p. 298.

4. Sharabi, *Palestine Guerrillas*, p. 45.

5. "An Interview with Fatah's Spokesman: Achievements of a Revolution 1965-1970," *Free Palestine* (Beirut) 1, no. 10 (February, 1970): 2.

6. "FBIS Daily Report," *Middle East & North Africa* V, no. 112 (July 15, 1974): A-3.

7. *FBIS-MEA*, 13 August 1974, p. A-3.

8. See: FBIS Daily Report, *Middle East & North Africa* V, no. 112 (2) (June 19, 1974): A6-7.

9. *Washington Post*, April 4, 1974, p. A-22.

10. Sharabi, *Palestine Guerrillas*, pp. 55-56.

11. William Quandt, Fuad Jabber, and Amy Lesch, *The Politics of Palestinian Nationalism* (Berkeley: University of California, 1973), p. 67.

12. "Abu Ammar Reviews Revolution Achievements, 1965-1970," *Fatah* 1, no. 7 (January 1, 1970), special issue; 3.

13. "Abu Ayyad at the American University," *An-Nahar* (in Arabic), November 29, 1969, p. 1.

14. Hisham Sharabi, *Palestine and Israel: The Lethal Dilemma* (New York: Pegasus, 1969), p. 198.

15. Barbara Wilson, *Palestinian Guerrilla Movements* (Washington, D.C.: The American University, Center for Research in Social Systems, 1969), p. 48.

16. "Towards the Democratic Palestine," *Fatah* II, no. 2 (January 19, 1970): 10.

17. Sharabi, *Palestine and Israel*, p. 201.

18. *Fatah* II, no. 2 (January 19, 1970): 10.

19. "The Democratic Front Says that Fatah Is a Bourgeois Government Apparatus," *An-Nahar*, December 24, 1969, p. 1; and "We Refuse the Marxist Ideology that is Being Imposed by Some of the Groups," *An-Nahar* (Sunday Supplement, in Arabic), March 22, 1970, p. 4.

20. Wilson, *Palestinian Guerrilla Movements*, p. 56.

21. *An-Nahar* (Sunday Supplement), March 22, 1970, p. 4.

22. Ibid.

23. *Fatah* (Special Issue), January 1, 1970, p. 2.

24. Ibid., p. 2.

25. Oriana Fallaci, "Fatah Chief Spells Out Hate of Israel," *Washington Post*, March 20, 1970, p. 82.

26. Sharabi, *Palestine Guerrillas*, p. 27.

27. "A Panel Discussion on Arab Guerrillas," *Free Palestine* 1, no. 10 (February 1970): 8.

28. Ibid.

Chapter 3
The Palestinian Movement and the Arab States

1. P.J. Vatikiotis, *Politics and the Military in Jordan: A Study of the Arab Legion 1921-1957* (New York: Frederick A. Praeger, 1967), p. 5.

2. Clinton Bailey, "Cabinet Formation in Jordan, 1950-1970," *New Outlook* 13, no. 8 (November 1970): 20.

3. Frederick Peake, *History and Tribes of Jordan* (Miami: The University of Miami Press, 1958), pp. 143-224 passim.

4. Bailey, "Cabinet Formation in Jordan," pp. 8-22.

5. Vatikiotis, *Politics and the Military in Jordan*, pp. 84-86 and 89-92.

6. Sir John Bagot Glubb, *A Soldier with the Arabs* (New York: Harper and Brothers Publishers, 1957), p. 279.

7. Vatikiotis, *Politics and the Military in Jordan*, p. 129, fn.

8. Ibid., p. 81.

9. Bailey, "Cabinet Formation in Jordan," p. 19.

10. Barbara Wilson, *Palestinian Guerrilla Movements* (Washington, D.C.: The American University, Center for Research in Social Systems, 1969), pp. 27-28.

11. "The Hundred Years' War," *The Economist* 233, no. 6584 (November 1, 1969): 14.

12. John Wolf, "Shadow on Lebanon," *Current History* 58, no. 341 (January 1970): 25.

13. Richard A. Falk, "The Beirut Raid and the International Law of Retaliation," *American Journal of International Law* 63, no. 3 (July 1969): 418.

14. "Mrs. Meir Warns Leaders in Beirut," *The New York Times*, August 13, 1969, p. 11.

15. Sam Pope Brewer, "Security Council Condemns Israel for Lebanon Raid," *The New York Times*, August 27, 1969, p. 1.

16. Dana Adams Schmidt, "Lebanese Stirred by a U.S. Statement," *The New York Times*, October 15, 1969, p. 5.

17. Ibid.

18. "Text of the Cairo Agreement," *An-Nahar* (in Arabic), April 20, 1970, p. 1.

19. Raymond Anderson, "Parley Took 7 Hours," *The New York Times,* November 4, 1969, p. 3.

20. "Lebanese Hail Accord," *The New York Times*, November 5, 1969, p. 2.

21. Alfred Friendly, Jr., "Prisoners Are Returned," *The New York Times*, November 6, 1969, p. 2.

22. Dana Adams Schmidt, "Beirut Bars Commandos in Two Towns," *The New York Times*, January 16, 1969, p. 8.

23. "Appeal of Fatah: The Palestinians Expect Complete Support from the Islamic Countries," *An-Nahar*, September 23, 1969, p. 1.

24. "Al Fatah Seeking to Explain Its Position to Lebanese Public," *The New York Times*, December 3, 1969, p. 12.

25. Ibid.

26. "Lebanon Imposes Curb on Funerals of Guerrillas," *The New York Times*, December 6, 1969, p. 3.

27. "Armed Commandos Stationed in Camps Have Left," *The New York Times*, December 7, 1969, p. 23.

28. "Guerrillas in 2 Arab Lands Apply Own Discipline," *The New York Times*, February 27, 1970, p. 3.

29. Dana Adams Schmidt, "Guerrillas Yield to Beirut's Plea," *The New York Times*, January 9, 1970, p. 9.

30. Dana Adams Schmidt, "Beirut Bans Commandos in Two Towns," *The New York Times*, January 16, 1970, p. 8.

31. Ibid.

32. *An-Nahar*, January 17, 1970, p. 10.

33. "Commandos Accuse Lebanon," *The New York Times*, January 12, 1970, p. 8.

34. "Reform Relocates Palestinians Inside Lebanon," *An-Nahar*, January 21, 1970, p. 1.

35. "Arafat in Damascus: There Is No Difference with Lebanon Concerning the Cairo Agreement and Many of the Palestinian Jews Are Interested in the Idea of a Collective State," *An-Nahar*, January 21, 1970, p. 6.

36. "Beirut Adopts Plan to Avoid Clashes with Commandos," *The New York Times*, March 21, 1970, p. 4.

37. "Guerrillas in 2 Arab Lands Apply Own Discipline," *The New York Times*.

38. "Beirut Adopts Plan to Avoid Clashes with Commandos," *The New York Times*.

39. "Fatah Calls for a New Evaluation of the Relations of Lebanon with the Fedayeen (Commandos). [The Congress] Will End Before the 15th of June and Will Not Act Upon the Cairo Agreement," *An-Nahar*, June 3, 1970, p. 1.

40. Dana Adams Schmidt, "Arab Guerrillas Elated, See Battle as a Victory," *The New York Times*, May 14, 1970, p. 3.

41. "Emigrants from the South Are 30 Thousand," *An-Nahar*, May 25, 1970, p. 1.

42. "Forbidding of Rocket Fire from Lebanese Territory," *An-Nahar*, May 28, 1970, p. 1.

43. "The Cairo Agreement Is Put to the Test Recently During a Session of the Cabinet," *An-Nahar*, June 15, 1970, p. 3.

44. "The Suggestion of the Minister of Works to the Cabinet About Lebanon's Relations with the Palestinian Resistance [Organization]," *An-Nahar*, June 6, 1970, p. 3.

45. "Lebanon Limits Arms-Carrying," *The New York Times*, June 15, 1969, p. 13.

46. John Cooley, "Jordan Clashes Shake Mideast Governments," *Christian Science Monitor*, October 20, 1970, p. 1.

47. Ibid.

48. "Arafat Arrives in Beirut; Guerrilla Purge Is Reported to be Aim," *The New York Times*, January 4, 1971, p. 3.

49. Eric Pace, "Arafat and Other Guerrilla Leaders Agree to Reorganize and to Seek Improved Relations with Beirut," *The New York Times*, November 1, 1970, p. 12.

50. "Arafat Arrives in Beirut," *The New York Times*.

51. *The Arab World*, June 29, 1972, pp. 11-12.

52. Ibid., December 12, 1971, p. 11.

53. *The New York Times*, December 9, 1972, p. 15.

54. *Washington Post*, May 18, 1973, p. A-22.

Chapter 4
The Rise of Terrorism

1. As translated in *The Arab World* (Beirut), September 17, 1973, p. 9.

2. The Arab World, May 31, 1972, p. 2.

3. Ibid., July 4, 1973, p. 12.

4. Ibid., August 16, 1973, p. 8.

5. *The New York Times*, April 12, 1974, p. 1.

6. *Washington Post*, May 16, 1974, p. 1.

7. *The New York Times*, July 2, 1974, p. 5.

Chapter 5
Conclusions and Outlook

1. Hisham Sharabi, *Palestine and Israel: The Lethal Dilemma* (New York: Pegasus, 1969), p. 186.

2. Ibid., p. 189.

3. Ibid., p. 187.

4. Barbara Wilson, *The Palestinian Guerrilla Movements* (Washington, D.C.: The American University, Center for Research in Social Systems, 1969), p. 24.

5. Ibid., p. 36.

6. Ibid., p. 32.

7. See: "Towards the Democratic Palestine," *Fatah* II, no. 2 (January 19, 1970), quoted in Paul Jureidini, *The Palestinian Revolution: Its Organization, Ideologies, and Dynamics* (Washington, D.C.: American Institutes for Research, May 1970), pp. 30-31.

8. Ibid., p. 31.

Bibliography

Bibliography of Selected References

General Sources

The Arab World (Beirut), 1968-74.
The Christian Science Monitor, July 1968-March 1974.
Falastin al-Thawra (Palestine Revolution), Beirut, July 1972.
Al-Hadaf (Beirut), July 1969—.
Al-Hurriyya (Beirut).
Journal of Palestine Studies.
An-Nahar (Beirut), 1968—.
An-Nahar Arab Report, 1968-74.
The New York Times, July 1968-March 1974.
Palestine Affairs (Arabic) (Beirut).
Washington Post, July 1968-March 1974.

Books and Pamphlets

Abbass, Abdul Majid. "Palestine (1933-1939)." *Challenge and Response in Internal Conflict*, Vol. II. Eds. D.M. Condit and Bert H. Cooper, Jr. Washington, D.C.: The American University, Center for Research in Social Systems, March 1967.

Abu-Lughod, Ibrahim (ed.). *The Transformation of Palestine*. Evanston: Northwestern University Press, 1971.

A Dialogue with Fatah. Interview with Salah Khalaf, Palestine National Liberation Movement, Fatah, Beirut, 1969.

al-'Azm, Sadiq Jalal. *Dirasa Naqdiya li Fikr al Muqawama al-Filastiniya* (A critical study of the thought of the Palestinian resistance). Bierut: Dar al-Auda, 1973.

al-'Adawi, Ibrahim Ahmad. *al-Sira' bayna al-Ummah al-'Arabiyah wa al-Isti'mar al-Jadid* (The struggle between the Arab nation and the new imperialism). Cairo: Dar Nahdat Misr, 1969.

al-Kayyali, Abd al-Wahhab (ed.). *A Modern History of Palestine* (in Arabic). Beirut: Arab Institute for Studies and Publication, 1970.

al-Khatib, Hussam. *Fi al-Tajriba al-Thawriya al-Filastiniya* (On the Palestinian revolutionary experience). Damascus: Ministry of Culture, 1972.

113

Allush, Naji. *Arab Resistance in Palestine*, 1914-1948 (in Arabic). Beirut: Palestine Research Center, 1967.

_____. *Ath-Thawra al-Filistiniyya: Ab'adaha wa Qadayaha* (The Palestinian Revolution: Its Aims and Problems). Beirut: Dar al-Tali'ah, 1970.

_____. *Manaqashat hawla al-Thawrah al- Filastiniyah* (Controversies about the Palestinian Revolution). Beirut: Dar al-Tali'ah, 1970.

al-Shibani, Karim. *Harakat al-Muqawamah* (The resistance movement). Beirut: al-Maktab al-Tijari, 1970.

Arey, J.F. *The Sky Pirates* New York: Scribner, 1972.

Aruri, Naseer (ed.). *The Palestinian Resistance Movement to Israel's Occupation*. Wilmette, Illinois Medina University Press, October 1970.

Ayoub, Sami (Khoury). *Al-Hisb al-Shuyu'e fi Suriya wa Lubnan* (The Communist Party in Syria and Lebanon: 1922-1958). Beirut: Printing and Publishing House, 1959.

Barron, John. *KGB: The Secret Work of Soviet Secret Agents*. New York: Reader's Digest Press, 1974.

Bell, J. Bowyer. *The Long War: Israel and the Arabs since 1946*. Englewood Cliffs, N.J.: Prentice-Hall, 1969.

_____. *The Myth of the Guerilla: Revolutionary Theory and Malpractice*. New York: Alfred Knopf, 1971.

Bentwich, Norman and Hellen. *Mandate Memoirs 1918-1948: From the Balfour Declaration to the Establishment of Israel*. New York: Schoken Books, 1956.

Black September. Beirut: P.L.O. Research Center, Palestine National Liberation Movement, Fatah, 1973.

Blechman, Barry. *The Consequences of the Israeli Reprisals: An Assessment*. Princeton: Princeton University Press, 1971.

Buchler, I.R., and H.G. Nutini (eds.). *Game Theory in the Behavioral Sciences*. Pittsburgh: University of Pittsburgh, 1969.

Carré, Oliver. *L'Idéologie Palestinienne de Résistance*. Paris: Colin, 1972.

Chaliand, Gerard. *The Palestinian Resistance*. Middlesex (England): Penguin Books, 1972.

Committee on Internal Security, U.S. House of Representatives, 93rd Congress, 1st Session, *Political Kidnappings 1968-1973*. Washington, D.C.: G.P.O., August 1, 1973.

Condit, D.M. *Modern Revolutionary Warfare: An Analytical Overview*. Washington, D.C.: American Institutes for Research, 1973.

Conquest, Robert. *Great Terror*. New York: MacMillan, 1973.

Cooley, John. *Green March, Black September.* London: Frank Carr, 1973.

Copeland, Miles. *The Game of Nations.* London: Weidenfeld and Nicolson, 1969.

Debray, Régis. *Révolution dans la Révolution? (Revolution in the Revolution?).* Paris: Libraire Français Maspero, 1967.

Denoyan, Gilbert. *El Fath Parle: Les Palestiniens contre Israél.* Paris: Editions Albin Michel, 1970.

Fawdah, "Izz al-Din. *al-Ihtilal al-Isra'ili wa al-Maqawamah al-Filastiniyah fi Daw' al-Qanun al-Duwali al'Amm* (Israeli occupation and Palestinian armed resistance in international law). Beirut: PLO Research Center, 1969.

Feierabend, Ivo, Rosalind L. Feierabend, and Ted R. Gurr (eds.). *Anger, Violence, and Politics: Theories and Research.* Englewood Cliffs, N.J.: Prentice-Hall, 1972.

For the Record—Intransigence Leads to Escalation: Who is Responsible? By the Arab League. London: The Arab League Office, 1971.

Francos, Ania. *Les Palestiniens.* Paris: Julliard, 1968.

Furlonge, Geoffrey. *Palestine Is My Country: The Story of Musa Alami.* London: John Murray, 1969.

George, A.L. *The "Operational Code": A Neglected Approach to the Study of Political Leaders and Decision Making.* Santa Monica: Rand Corporation, 1967.

Gross, Feliks. *Violence in Politics: Terror and Political Assassination in Eastern Europe and Russia.* The Hague, the Netherlands: Mouton, 1973.

Gurr, Ted R. *Why Men Rebel.* Princeton: Princeton University Press, 1970.

Haikal, Yusuf, *Filastin: Qabl wa Ba'd* (Palestine Before and After). Beirut: Dar al-'Ilm lil-Malayin, 1971.

Hammond, Paul Y., and Sidney S. Alexander (eds.). *Political Dynamics in the Middle East.* New York: American Elsevier, 1972.

Harkabi, Yehoshafat. *Arab Attitudes to Israel.* New York: Hart, 1972.

———. *Fedayeen Action and Arab Strategy.* Adelphi Papers, No. 53. London: Institute for Strategic Studies, December 1968.

———. *The Position of the Palestinians in the Israel-Arab Conflict and Their National Covenant* (1968). Trans. J. Kraemer. Jerusalem, 1970.

Harkabi, Yehoshafat, Elizabeth Monroe, Fayez A. Sayegh, and John Coventry Smith. *Time Bomb in the Middle East.* New York: Friendship Press, 1969.

Hobeychi, General Abdallah. *The Palestine Problem*. Damascus: al-Tawjih Press, 1971.

Horowitz, Irving L. *Political Terrorism and Personal Deviance*. Washington, D.C.: Department of State, External Research Study, February 15, 1973.

_____. (ed.). *The Anarchists*. New York: Dell Publishing Company, 1964.

Hubbard, David. *The Skyjacker*. New York: Collier Books, 1973.

Institute for Palestine Studies and the Arab Women's Information Committee. *Who are the Terrorists? Aspects of Zionist and Israeli Terrorism*. 1972 Monograph Series, No. 33.

International Documents on Palestine, 1967 and 1968. Beirut: Institute for Palestine Studies, 1970 and 1971.

International Terrorism: An Annotated Bibliography. Santa Monica: The Rand Corporation, September 1973.

Ismael, Tareq Y. (ed.). *The Middle East in World Politics*. Syracuse: Syracuse University Press, 1974.

Jabhat al-Tahrir al-'Arabiyah. *al-Tariq al-Qawmi li-Tahrir Filastin* (The nationalist way to liberating Palestine). Beirut: Dar al-Tali'ah, 1970.

Jabr, Muhammad. *Murasil Harbi fi al-Jahhah* (On military activities since the June 1967 war). Cairo: Dar al-Ta'awun, 1971.

Jansen, Michael. *The United States and the Palestinian People*. Beirut: Institute for Palestine Studies, 1968.

Jansen, Godfrey. *Why Robert Kennedy was Killed: The Story of Two Victims*. New York: The Third Press, 1971.

Jureidini, Paul A. *The Palestinian Revolution: Its Organizations, Ideologies, and Dynamics*. Washington, D.C.: Center for Research in Social Systems, 1970.

Kadi, Leila. *Basic Political Documents of the Armed Palestinian Resistance Movement*. Beirut: Palestine Liberation Organization, Research Centre, 1969.

Kerr, Malcolm H. *The Arab Cold War: Gamal 'Abd al-Nasir and His Rivals, 1958-1970*. 3rd ed. New York: Oxford University Press, 1971.

Khaled, Leila. *My People Shall Live: The Autobiography of a Revolutionary*. (Edited by George Hajjar). London: Hodder and Stoughton, 1973.

Khouri, Fred J. *The Arab-Israeli Dilemma*. Syracuse, New York. Syracuse University Press, 1968.

Kirk, George E. *A Short History of the Middle East*. New York: Frederick A. Praeger, 1955.

Kishk, Muhammad Jalal. *al-Thawrah al-Filastiniyah* (The Palestinian Revolution). Beirut: Matabi' Ma'tuq Ikhwan, 1970.

Laffin, John. *Fedayeen: The Arab-Israeli Dilemma*. New York: Free Press, 1973.

La Révolution palestinienne et les juifs. By Fatah. Paris: Editions de minuit, 1970.

Leites, N.C., and C. Wolf, Jr. *Rebellion and Authority: An Analytic Essay on Insurgent Conflicts*. Chicago: Markham Publishing Co., 1970.

L'Idéologie Palestinienne de Résistance: analyse de textes 1964-1970. No. 20 Traveux et Recherches de Science Politique of the Fondation Nationale des Sciences Politiques.

Little, Tom. *The New Arab Extremists: A view from the Arab World*. London: Current Affairs Research Services Centre, 1970. Conflict Studies No. 4.

Mujdhub, Muhammad. *A'mal Isra'il al-Intiqamiyah didda al-Duwal al-'Arabiyah* (Israeli reprisals against Arab countries). Beirut: PLO Research Center, 1970.

Murqass, Elias. *Al-Muqawama al-Filastiniya wa al-Mawqif al-Rahin* (The Palestinian resistance and the present situation). Beirut: Dar al Haqiqa, 1971.

On the Crisis of the Palestinian Resistance Movement (in Arabic). Documents submitted by the PDFLP to the Sixth National Congress, September 1969. Beirut: Dar al-Tali'ah, 1970.

Palestine Lives. Beirut: Palestine Research Center and Kuwaiti Teachers Association, 1973.

Palestine National Liberation Movement, The (al-Fatah). *Watha'iq 'Askariyya* (military documents). Amman: Al-Fatah, 1968.

Peretz, Don, Evan Wilson, and Richard J. Ward (eds.). *A Palestine Entity?* Special Study Number One. Washington, D.C.: The Middle East Institute, 1970.

Political Armed Struggle. The Palestine National Liberation Movement, Fatah. Beirut: 1970.

Popular Democratic Front for the Liberation of Palestine, The (Introduction by Nayef Hawatmeh). *Harakat al-Muqawama al-Filistiniyya fi Waqi'iha ar-Rahin. . .* (The Present State of the Palestinian Resistance Movement—a critical study). Beirut: Dar al-Tali'ah, 1969.

Proche-Orient: de la Résistance Palestinienne à la révolution socialiste. Published by Jeune garde socialiste. Paris: Maspero, 1970.

Quandt, William B. *Palestinian Nationalism: Its Political and Military Dimensions*. Santa Monica: The Rand Corporation, 1971.

Quandt, William B., Fuad Jabber, and Ann Mosely Lesch. *The Politics of Palestinian Nationalism*. Berkeley: University of California Press, 1973.

Rao, Sudha V. *The Arab-Israeli Conflict: The Indian View*. New Delhi: Orient Longman, 1972.

Revolution until Victory. The Palestine National Liberation Movement, Fatah. Beirut, 1970.

Rodinson, Maxime. *Israel and the Arabs* (revised edition with postscript), London and Baltimore: Penguin Books, 1970.

Sayegh, Anis. *Palestine Chronology*, Vols. I-XI. January 1, 1965 to June 30, 1970. Beirut: Research Centre. Palestine Liberation Organization.

Schiff, Zeev, and Raphael Rothstein. *Fedayeen: Guerrilla Against Israel*. New York: McKay, 1972.

Sharabi, Hisham. *Arab Intellectuals and the West: The Formative Years, 1875-1914*. Baltimore: Johns Hopkins Press, 1970.

_____. *Palestine and Israel: The Lethal Dilemma*. New York: Pegasus, 1969.

_____. *Palestine Guerrillas: Their Credibility and Effectiveness*. Washington, D.C.: Center for Strategic and International Studies, Georgetown University, Supplementary Papers, 1970.

Shukayri, Ahmad. *al-Nizam al-Urduni fi Qafas al-Ittiham* (Speeches delivered in February 1972 before the Egyptian Court for the Case of Wasfi al-Tall's Assassination in Cairo, November 28, 1971, with Emphasis on Palestinian-Jordan Relations). Cairo: Dar Hiradut lil-taba'ah wa al-Nashr wa al-Tawzi'a, 1972.

Snow, Peter, and David Phillips. *Leila's Hijack War*. London: Pan Books, 1970.

_____. *The Arab Hijack War: The True Story of 25 Days in September 1970*. New York: Ballantine, 1971.

Stetler, Russel (ed.). *Palestine: The Arab-Israeli Conflict*. Los Angeles: Ramparts Press, 1972.

Stock, Ernest. *Israel on the Road to Sinai*. Ithaca: Cornell University Press, 1967.

Sykes, Christopher. *Crossroads to Israel*. Cleveland: The World Publishing Company, 1965.

The Future of Palestine. Beirut: Hermon Books, 1970.

Tomeh, George. *Legal Status of Arab Refugees*. Beirut: The Institute for Palestine Studies, 1969.

Tuma, Elias H. *Peacemaking and the Immoral War: Arabs and Jews in the Middle East*. New York: Harper, 1972.

Turki, Fawaz. *The Disinherited: Journal of a Palestine Exile*. New York: Monthly Review Press, 1972.

Vatikiotis, P.J. *Conflict in the Middle East*. London: George Allen and Unwin Ltd., 1971.

_____. (ed.). *Revolution in the Middle East and Other Case Studies*. George Allen and Unwin Ltd., 1972.

Verges, Jacques M. *Pour les Fidayine*. Paris: Les Editions de Minuit, 1969.

Walter, Eugene. *Terror and Resistance: A Study of Political Violence*. New York: Oxford University Press, 1969.

Wilson, Barbara. *Palestinian Guerrilla Movements*. Washington, D.C.: The American University, Center for Research in Social Systems, 1969.

Yaari, Ehud. *Strike Terror: The Story of Fatah*. New York: Amis Publishing Co., 1971.

Yahalom, Yiftah. *Le Terrorisme Arabe*. Tel Aviv: Mouvement Ouvrier Sioniste Mondial, 1969.

Young, Oran R. *The Intermediaries: Third Parties in International Crises*. Princeton: Princeton University Press, 1967.

_____. *The Politics of Force: Bargaining During International Crises*. Princeton: Princeton University Press, 1967.

Articles and Papers

Abosch, H. "Un Coup d'Arret dans les Relations Germano-Arabes," *Le Monde Diplomatique*, No. 223 (October 1972), p. 8.

Abou, Leila. "Diriger la révolution nationale democratique," *Eléments*, Nos. 8-9 (1971-1972), pp. 87-91.

"Abu Ammar Reviews Revolution Achievements, 1965-1970," *Fatah*, Vol. I, No. 7, Special Issue (January 1, 1970).

"Abu-Ammar Speaks," *Free Palestine* (Washington), Vol. 2, No. 10 (February, 1971), pp. 1-2.

Abu-Jaber, Faiz S. "Soviet Attitude Toward Arab Revolutions: Yemen, Egypt, Algeria, Iraq and Palestine," *Middle East Forum*, Vol. 64, No. 4 (1970), pp. 41-65.

Abu Jabir, K. "Ideology, the Arab Intelligentsia, and the Palestinian Cause and Question" (in Arabic), *Dirasat 'Arabiya*, Vol. 5, No. 8 (1969), pp. 32-43.

Abu-Lughod, I. "Altered Realities: The Palestinians Since 1967," *International Journal*, Vol. 28, No. 4 (1973), pp. 648-69.

Abu 'Umar. "The Arab Revolution and the World Revolution" (in Arabic), *Shu'un Filastiniya* (Beirut), No. 17 (January 1973), pp. 30-36.

'Adwan, K. "An Analysis of the Political Situation" (in Arabic), *Shu'un Filastiniya* (Beirut), No. 11 (July 1972), pp. 274-81.

Aggarwala, N. "Political Aspects of Hijacking," *International Conciliation*, No. 858 (July 1972), pp. 7-27.

Aksentijevic, M. "The Crisis in Jordan," *Review International Affairs*, Vol. 21, No. 492 (October 1970), pp. 6-8.

Al-Ayyubi, H. "Guide to Researchers: Fatah's Political and Military Ideas" (in Arabic), *Shu'un Filastiniya* (Beirut), No. 29 (January 1974), pp. 116-26.

_____. "The Material Consequences of the Fourth War on the Stage of Operations" (in Arabic), *Dirasat 'Arabiya*, Vol. 10, No. 4 (February 1974), pp. 12-27.

_____. "Palestine Resistance in the Phase of Flexible and Dynamic Defence" (in Arabic), *Shu'un Filastiniya* (Beirut), No. 19 (March 1973), pp. 28-34.

Alexander, Y. "The religionation of the Middle East conflict by some Moslem groups outside the area," *International Problems*, Vol. 11, Nos. 3-4 (December 1972), pp. 16-22.

Al-Fattal, R.K. "Palestine Liberation Movement," *Islamic Review*, Vol. 57, No. 6 (June 1969), pp. 33-36.

Al-Hasan, B., et al. "Political Assassination and the Revolution: A Panel" (in Arabic), *Dirasat 'Arabiya*, Vol. 8, No. 3 (Janaury 1972), pp. 2-6, 151-66.

Al-Hasan, H. "Fatah between Theory and Practice: The Theoretical Framework" (in Arabic), *Shu'un Filastiniya* (Beirut), No. 7 (March 1972), pp. 9-21.

Allush, N. "The Palestinian Revolution and the Tasks Before the Arab Liberation Movement" (in Arabic), *Dirasat 'Arabiya*, No. 8, (June 1972), pp. 9-16.

_____. "The People's War . . . and the Arab People's War" (in Arabic), *Dirasat 'Arabiya*, No. 12 (October 1973), pp. 105-10.

_____. "Towards a New Stage in the Palestinian Revolution" (in Arabic), *Dirasat 'Arabiya*, No. 7 (May 1973), pp. 2-3.

Al-Mulatham, B. "Men of Thought in Palestine: A. 'Ata Allah and 'A. al-Qadir al-Hasini" (in Arabic), *al-'Adib*, No. 11 (November 1969) pp. 2-5.

_____. "Men of Thought in Palestine: A. al-Khalidi and Z. al-Karami," (in Arabic), *al'Adib* No. 12 (December 1969), pp. 28-33.

Al-Qadi, L. "A Review of the Peaceful Settlement Schemes of the Arab-Israeli Conflict, 1948-1972" (in Arabic), *Shu'un Filastiniya* (Beirut), No. 22 (July 1973), pp. 84-123.

Al-Qawuqji, F. "Memoirs, 1948: I," *Journal of Palestine Studies*, Vol. 1, No. 4 (1972), pp. 27-58.

Amin, W. "The National Movement in the Face of Imperialist Plans" (in Arabic), *al-Tali'ah*, Vol. 8, No. 4 (April 1972), pp. 20-29.

'A., N. "Opinion: Toward a Constructive Debate of the Palestine resistance Movement" (in Arabic), *Shu'un Filastiniya* (Beirut), No. 6 (January 1972), pp. 5-17.

Anabtawi, S.N. "The Palestinians as a Political Entity," *Muslim World*, Vol. 60, No. 1 (January 1970), pp. 47-58.

"An Interview with Fatah's Spokesman: Achievements of a Revolution: 1965-1970," *Free Palestine*, Vol. 1, No. 10 (February 1970).

"A Panel Discussion on Arab Guerrillas," *Free Palestine*, Vol. 1, No. 10 (February 1970), p. 8.

"Arab Documents on Palestine, November 15, 1971-February 15, 1972," *Journal of Palestine Studies*, Vol. 1, No. 3 (1972), pp. 158-74.

Ashhab, N. "To overcome crisis of Palestine resistance movement," *World Marxist Review*, Vol. 15, No. 5 (May 1972), pp. 71-78.

"Attacks on Palestinians," *Middle East International*, No. 20 (February 1973), pp. 20-23.

'Azam, S. "Armed resistance and organizational framework" (in Arabic), *Dirasat 'Arabiya* Vol. 5, No. 10 (1969), pp. 17-36.

Bahra, N. "Towards consolidating the Palestine cause" (in Arabic), *Sawt Filastin*, No. 51 (April 1972), pp. 89-100.

Balta, P. "Le Proche-Orient après Munich," *Le Monde Diplomatique*, No. 223 (October 1972), pp. 1, 6.

Bassiouni, C., and E. Fisher. "An Arab-Israeli Conflict: Real and Apparent Issues, an Insight into Its Future from the Lessons of the Past," *St. John's Law Review*, Vol. 44 (1970), pp. 399-465.

Batal, G. "Main Long-Term Trends in the National Liberation Movement" (in Arabic), *al-Tariq* (Beirut), No. 9 (October 1972), pp. 27-35.

Beit-Hallahmi, B. "Some Psycho-Social-Cultural Factors in the Arab-Israeli Conflict: A Review of the Literature," *Journal of Conflict Resolution*, Vol. 16, No. 2 (July 1972), pp. 269-80.

Benguigui, G. "Le Gauchisme et les Palestiniens" *Les Nouveau Cahiers*, No. 33 (Summer 1973), pp. 22-28.

Ben Porat, Y. "The Secret Warriors," *Israel Magazine*, Vol. 5, No. 1 (January 1973), pp. 37-42.

Berri, Y. "La vengeance qui vient du ciel," *Jeune Afrique*, No. 611 (September 23, 1972), pp. 14-18.

_____. "Leur morale et la votre," *Jeune Afrique*, No. 597 (July 17, 1972) pp. 35-37.

Bichara, K. "La résistance palestinienne," *Revue Nouvelle*, September 1970, pp. 161-76.

Blechman, B. "The Impact of Israel's Reprisals on Behavior of the Bordering Arab Nations Directed at Israel," *Journal of Conflict Resolution*, Vol. 16, No. 2 (July 1972), pp. 155-82.

Blum, Yehuda Z. "The Beirut Raid and the International Double Standard," *American Journal of International Law*, Vol. 64, No. 1 (January 1970), 73-105.

Bowett, O. "Reprisals Involving Recourse to Armed Force," *American Journal of International Law*, January 1972, pp. 1-36.

Boyce, F. "The Internationalizing of Internal War: Ethiopia, the Arabs, and the Case of Eritrea," *Journal of International and Comparative Studies*, Vol. 5, No. 3 (1972), pp. 51-73.

Brewer, Sam Pope. "Security Council Condemns Israel for Lebanon Raid," *The New York Times*, August 27, 1969, p. 1.

Campbell, J. "The Arab-Israeli Conflict: An American policy," *Foreign Affairs*, Vol. 49 (October 1970), pp. 51-69.

Carré, O. "The Palestinian Response to the Israeli Challenge: Legend, Utopia and Ideology" (in Arabic), *Shu'un Filastiniya* (Beirut), No. 6 (January 1972), pp. 31-44.

Chaliand, Gerard. "Palestine: la résistance, son idéologie et ses tendences," *Le Monde Diplomatique*, No. 230 (May 1973), p. 26.

_____. "Le Double Combat du F.P.L.P.," *Le Monde Diplomatique*, July 1970.

_____. "Terrorisme et Politique," *Le Monde Diplomatique*, No. 230 (May 1973), p. 24.

Cheney, J., L. Harford, and L. Solomon. "The Effects of Communication Threats and Promises upon the Bargaining Process," *Journal of Conflict Resolution*, Vol. 16, No. 1 (March 1972), pp. 99-107.

"Chronology of Zionist and Israeli Terrorism," *Palestine Digest*, Vol. 2, No. 10 (January 1973), pp. 3-8.

"Civil War in Jordan," *Mid East*, Vol. 10, No. 6 (December 1970), pp. 21-24.

Cooley, J. "China and the Palestinians," *Journal of Palestine Studies*, Vol. 1, No. 2 (1972), pp. 19-34.

_____. "Moscow faces a Palestinian Dilemma," *Mid East*, Vol. 10, No. 3 (June 1970), pp. 32-35.

Carvely, A. "Libya: International Relations and Political Purposes" *International Journal*, Vol. 28, No. 4 (1973), pp. 707-28.

de Silva, Mervyn. "Cool, Young Breed Inherits Arab Terror Movement," *The Ottowa Citizen*, December 27, 1968, p. 7.

Domenach, J.M. "Terrorism" (in Arabic), *Al-Haq*, No. 2 (May, 1973), pp. 72-75.

Dorsey, W.H., Jr. "Arab commandos," *New Republic*, 161 No. 21 (November 22, 1969), pp. 19-22.

El-Ayouty, Yassin. "The Palestinians and the Fourth Arab-Israeli War," *Current History*, Vol. 66, No. 390 (February 1974), pp. 74-78.

El-Azim, S. "Le Mouvement de Résistance reste handicap par ses réflexes hérites de la petite-bourgeoisie," *Le Monde Diplomatique*, No. 217 (April 1972), p. 9.

Entelis, J. "Palestinian revolutionism—Lebanese politics: The Christian response," *Muslim World*, Vol. 62, No. 4 (October 1972), pp. 335-51.

Ericsson, B. "The Palestinian movement and Israeli counteractions," *Internasional Politikk*, No. 1 (1969), pp. 45-53.

Evans, Alona. "Aircraft Hijacking: What is Being Done," *American Journal of International Law*, Vol. 67, No. 4 (October, 1973), pp. 641-71.

———. "Terrorism and Political Crimes in International Law," (Proceedings of the 67th Annual Meeting), *American Society of International Law*, April 12-14, 1973, pp. 87-111.

Eytan, E. "Les Héros sont Fatigués," *L'Arabe*, No. 184 (June-July 1972), pp. 37-41.

———. "Les Terroristes Arabes en Europe," *L'Arabe*, No. 186-87 (September-October, 1972), pp. xiv-xvi.

———. "Vienne: Le Seder des Juifs de l'URSS," *L'Arabe*, No. 196 (May 26-June 25, 1973), pp. 47-50.

Falk, Richard A. "The Beirut Raid and the International Law of Retaliation," *American Journal of International Law*, Vol. 63, No. 3 (July 1969), pp. 415-43.

Fallaci, Oriana. "Fatah Chief Spells Out Hate of Israel," *Washington Post*, March 20, 1970, p. B2.

"Fatah: Its Emergence and Progress. An Interview with Kamel 'Adwan" (in Arabic), *Shu'un Filastiniya* (Beirut), No. 17 (January 1973).

Feiler, E. "The Terror of the Crime of Munich," *Israel at Peace*, No. 8 (September 1972), pp. 1-4.

Feron, James. "Allon Says Israel Will Act if Armies Invade Lebanon," *The New York Times*, October 25, 1969, p. 1.

Forsythe, David P. "The Soviets and the Arab-Israeli Conflict," *World Affairs*, Vol. 134, No. 2 (Fall, 1971), pp. 132-42.

Francos, A. "Beyrouth: La nuit des longs couteaux," *Jeune Afrique*, No. 641 (April 21, 1973), pp. 39-41.

_____. "Nous n'avons pas tué," *Jeune Afrique*, No. 615 (October 1972), pp. 12-16.

_____. "Palestine: la résistance a bout de souffle?," *Jeune Afrique*, No. 525 (January 26, 1971), pp. 42-45.

_____. "Résistance Palestine dans la résistance," *Jeune Afrique*, No. 532 (March 16, 1971), pp. 39-43.

Franjieh, S. "How Revolutionary Is the Palestinian Resistance? A Marxist Interpretation," *Journal of Palestine Studies*, Vol. 1, No. 2 (1972), pp. 52-60.

_____. "Les Pays Arabes Visent à Empêcher La Naissance d'un Parti Palestinien Révolutionnaire," *Le Monde Diplomatique*, No. 219 (June 1972), p. 5.

_____. "Tourrant dans l'Activité de la Résistance Palestinienne?," *Le Monde Diplomatique*, No. 223 (October 1972), pp. 6-7.

Franck, T.M., and Bert B. Lockwood, Jr. "Preliminary Thoughts towards an International Convention on Terrorism," *American Journal of International Law*, Vol. 681, No. 1 (January 1974), pp. 68-90.

Friendly, A., Sr. "The Middle East: The Fedayeen," *Atlantic Monthly*, Vol. 224, No. 3 (September 1969), pp. 12-20.

Fulbright, J. "The Middle East: Perspectives for Peace," *Survival*, Vol. 12, No. 11 (November 1970), pp. 360-68.

Gendzier, I.L. "Lebanon and the Palestinians," *New Outlook*, Vol. 12, No. 2 (February 1969), pp. 22-27.

_____. "The Palestinian Revolution, Palestine, Fatah, the Jews, and Other Matters," *New Middle East*, Vol. 28 (January 1971), pp. 38-41.

Genet, Jean. "The Palestinians," *Journal of Palestine Studies*, Vol. 3, No. 1 (Autumn 1973), pp. 3-34.

Ghareeb, E. "Munich and Beyond," *Arab Palestinian Resistance*, Vol. 4, No. 10 (October 1972), pp. 39-43.

Ghazzi, U. "The Syrian Communist Party Crisis and the Palestinian Cause: A Comparative Study with Some Arab Communist Parties" (in Arabic), *Shu'un Filastiniya* (Beirut), No. 12 (August 1972), pp. 128-37.

Ghilan, M. "Is There a Black September?" *Israel and Palestine*, No. 16-17 (December 1972-January 1973), pp. 1-2.

Goldman, Nahum. "The Future of Israel," *Foreign Affairs*, Vol. 48, No. 3 (April 1970), pp. 443-59.

Gottlieb, Gidon. "China and the Middle East," *Middle East Information Series*, Vol. 18 (April 1972), pp. 2-10.

Grant, Z.B. "Commando Revolution: A Hundred Years' War in the Middle East?" *New Republic*, Vol. 162, No. 4 (January 24, 1970), pp. 9-11.

Haddad, W. "Jordan's Civil War of 1970-71 in Historical Perspective," *Illinois Quarterly*, Vol. 34, No. 1 (September 1971), pp. 43-53.

Halliday, F. "An Interview with Ghassan Kannafani on the PFLP and the September Attack," *New Left Review*, No. 67 (May-June 1971), pp. 47-57.

Handman, J.B.S. "Terrorism," *The Encyclopedia of Social Sciences*, Vol. 14, (1937), pp. 575-80.

Harkabi, Yehoshafat. "Fedayeen Action and Arab Strategy," *Midstream*, Vol. 15, No. 5 (May 1969), pp. 14-22.

Harrington, M. "The New Left and the Arab-Israeli Conflict," *Current* No. 118 (May 1970), pp. 23-27.

"Has Fatah Become 'Moderate'? Abu Ammar Interview," *Free Palestine*, Vol. 2, No. 4 (1970), pp. 1 ff.

Hawatemeh, N. (interview). "Definitions of a Battle," *Tricontinental*, Vol. 31 (July-August 1972), pp. 94-110.

Hermann, K. "Reason from the Barrel of a Gun: In Action with Arab Commandos," *Atlas*, Vol. 19, No. 5 (1970), pp. 23-25.

Herodstveit, D. "Arab Demands and Desires in the Conflict with the State of Israel," *New Outlook*, Vol. 16, No. 7 (September 1973), pp. 22-30.

Horowitz, Irving L. "Political Terrorism and State Power," *Journal of Political and Military Sociology*, Vol. 1 (Spring 1973), pp. 147-57.

Hottinger, A. "The Fedayeen in Jordan," *Swiss Review World Affairs*, Vol. 20, No. 6 (September 1970), pp. 15-19.

"How American Radicals See the Resistance Dilemma," *Journal of Palestine Studies*, Vol. 1, No. 4 (Summer 1972), pp. 3-26.

Howard, H. "Jordan in Turmoil," *Current History*, Vol. 62, No. 365 (January 1972), pp. 14-19.

Howard, N.F. "Jordan: The Commando State," *Current History*, Vol. 58, No. 341 (Janaury 1970), pp. 8-12.

Hudson, Michael. "Fedayeen Are Forcing Lebanon's Hand," *Mid East*, Vol. 10, No. 1 (February 1970), pp. 7-15.

———. "The Palestinian Arab Resistance: Its Significance in the Middle East Crisis," *Middle East Journal*, Vol. 23, No. 3 (Summer 1969), pp. 291-307.

Husayn, G.H. "Hostility to the Arabs in West Germany" (in Arabic), *Sawt Filastin*, No. 9 (March 1973), pp. 33-48.

———. "West German and Israeli Responsibility for the Munich Incident" (in Arabic), *al-Tala'i' wa al-Jamahir*, No. 17 (October 1972), pp. 3-6.

Hutchinson, M. "The Concept of Revolutionary Terrorism," *Journal of Conflict Resolution*, Vol. 16, No. 3 (1972), pp. 383-97.

Hyman, A. "Interview with Jamil Hamad, a Palestinian," *New Outlook*, Vol. 14, No. 7 (September 1971), pp. 40-44.

Ismael, T. "The Palestinian Emergence and U.S. Foreign Policy," *Middle East Forum*, Vol. 46, Nos. 2-3 (1970), pp. 65-72.

"Israel's Counter-Terror," *Israel and Palestine*, No. 19 (March 1973), pp. 1-9.

Jabber, F. "The Arab regimes and the Palestinian Revolution, 1967-71," *Journal of Palestine Studies*, Vol. 2, No. 2 (1973), pp. 79-101.

"Jews and Arabs: When all Are Brothers," *The Economist*, Vol. 235, No. 6602 (March 7, 1970), p. 30.

Johnson, P. "Palestinian Movement Debates Response to Moves for Imposed Political Settlement," *MERIP Reports*, No. 15 (March 1973), p. 27.

Jones, D. "Reprisal: Israeli style," *Military Review*, Vol. 50, No. 8 (August 1970), pp. 91-96.

Joseph, L. "Tactics of Terror," *Lillit* (Jerusalem), No. 12 (October 1972), pp. 23-24.

Kanafani, Gh. "Dialectique de la Révolution Arabe," *Elements*, Nos. 8-9 (1971-72), pp. 79-86.

———. "The 1936-1939 Revolution in Palestine: The Background, Details and Analysis" (in Arabic), *Shu'un Filastiniya* (Beirut), No. 6 (January 1972), pp. 45-77.

Kapeliuk, A. "Lebanon's Hour of Trial," *New Outlook*, Vol. 12, No. 9 (November-December 1969), pp. 7-16.

Karber, Phillip. "Organizational Vulnerabilities of Terror Mounts." Paper presented before D.C. Political Science Association, May 1973.

Kelidar, Abbas. "The Palestine Guerrilla Movement," *The World Today*, Vol. 29, No. 10 (October 1973), pp. 412-20.

Khalis, M. "L'espoir des désespérés," *Jeune Afrique*, No. 610 (September 16, 1972), pp. 19-22.

Khan, R.A. "Lebanon at the Crossroads," *World Today*, Vol. 25, No. 12 (December 1969), pp. 530-36.

Khatib, Dr. Hasan. "Thoughts on Palestinian Violence" (in Arabic), *Shu'un Filastiniya* (Beirut), No. 7 (March 1972), pp. 22-26.

Krammer, A. "Soviet Motives in the Partition of Palestine, 1957-58," *Journal of Palestine Studies*, Vol. 2, No. 2 (1973), pp. 102-19.

Kuroda, Y. "Young Palestinian Commandos in Political Socialization Perspective," *Middle East Journal*, Vol. 26, No. 3 (1972), pp. 253-70.

"La résistance Palestinienne après cessez-le-feu," *Jeune Afrique*, No. 505 (September 8, 1970), pp. 16-22.

"L'avenir d'Israel," *Preuves*, No. 5 (1971), pp. 17-23.

"Lebanon and the Lod Massacre," *Israel Horizons*, Vol. 20, Nos. 5 and 6 (March-June 1972), pp. 3-4.

Lenczowski, G. "Arab Radicalism: Problems and Prospects," *Current History*, Vol. 60, No. 353 (January 1971), pp. 32-37 ff.

"Le peuple palestinien en marche," *Partisans* (March-April 1970), pp. 5-19.

"Les comités de Palestine et les Gauchistes" *Est et Ouest*, Vol. 21, No. 435 (November 16-30, 1969), pp. 10-12.

"Libya's Foreign Adventures," *Conflict Studies*, No. 41 (December 1973), pp. 1-16.

Little, S. "Fedayeen: Palestinian Commandos," *Military Review*, Vol. 50, No. 11 (November 1970), pp. 49-55.

Little, T. "The Nature of the Palestine Resistance Movement," *Royal Central Asian Journal*, Vol. 57, Pt. 2 (1970), pp. 157-69.

Loomis, C.P. "In Praise of Conflict and Its Resolution," *American Sociological Review*, Vol. 32, No. 6 (December 1967), pp. 875-90.

Louvish, M. "The Battle of Lydda," *Jewish Frontier*, Vol. 39, No. 5 (June 1972), pp. 7-9.

———. "The Meaning of Black September," *Jewish Frontier*, 39, No. 8 (October 1972), pp. 6-8.

Mallison, Jr., W.T., and S.V. Mallison. "The Juridical Characteristics of the Palestinian Resistance: An Appraisal in International Law," *Journal of Palestine Studies*, Vol. 2 No. 2 (Winter 1973), pp. 64-78.

Mansur, F. "Palestinian Resistance in the British, German and American Press 1966-71" (in Arabic), *Shu'un Filastiniya* (Beirut), No. 6 (January 1972), pp. 78-103.

Maqsud, Dr. Clovis. "Features of Arab Participation in the Palestinian Revolution" (in Arabic), *Shu'un Filastiniya* (Beirut), No. 10 (June 1972), pp. 5-31.

Mazrui, Ali A. "The Contemporary Case for Violence." *Civil Violence and the International System. Part I: The Scope of Civil Violence* (Adelphi Papers No. 82), London: The International Institute for Strategic Studies, 1971.

Mertz, R. "Why George Habash turned Marxist," *Mid East*, Vol. 10, No. 4 (1970), pp. 31-36.

M.L. "Après Munich" *Droit et Liberté*, No. 314 (September-October 1972), pp. 4-6.

"Mohammed Yazid on Algeria and the Arab-Israeli Conflict," *Journal of Palestine Studies*, Vol. 1, No. 2 (Winter 1972), pp. 1-18.

Morris, C. "Report on Jordan," *Middle East International*, No. 6 (September 1971), pp. 13-16.

Mroue, K. "A Critical Period: The Arab National Liberation Movement at the Present Time" (in Arabic) *Al-Waqt*, No. 2 (February 1973), pp. 44-48.

_____. "Arab National Liberation Movement," *World Marxist Review* Vol. 16, No. 2 (February 1973), pp. 65-72.

_____. "On Lebanese-Palestinian Relations" (in Arabic), *Shu'un Filastiniya* (Beirut), No. 23 (July 1973), pp. 12-16.

_____. "The Arab Liberation Movement," *World Marxist Review*, Vol. 15, No. 10 (October 1972), pp. 121-23.

Nahmias, H. and D. "Arab and Israeli Attitudes toward Authority," *International Problems*, Vol. 11, Nos. 3-4 (December 1972), pp. 23-26.

Nakhleh, Emile A. "The Anatomy of Violence: Theoretical Reflections on Palestinian Resistance," *Middle East Journal*, Vol. 25, No. 2 (Spring 1971), pp. 180-200.

"National Unity Is Our Principal Demand," *Fatah* (Arab Version), January 26, 1970, p. 5.

N'Diaye, J.P. "Pourquoi Khartoum?" *Jeune Afrique*, No. 636 (March 17, 1973), pp. 2-5.

Nicola, E. "Why the Palestinians Were Hunted (Palestinian Students in Germany after the Munich Affair)," *Israel and Palestine*, No. 15 (November 1972), pp. 1-2.

O'Ballance, E. "Israeli Counter-Guerrilla Measures," *J.R. United Services Institutes for Defence Studies*, No. 117 (March 1972), pp. 47-52.

Olson, Robert. "International Terrorism: Turkey." Paper delivered at the Seventh Annual meeting of the Middle East Studies Association at Milwaukee, November 8-10, 1973.

"On the Arab-Israeli Conflict," *Reconciliation Quarterly*, (1970), pp. 4-23 ff.

Pace, E. "The Violent Men of Amman," *New York Times Magazine*, July 19, 1970, pp. 8-9 ff.

Pa'il, M. "The Moral Use of Arms," *New Outlook*, 16, No. 2 (February 1973), pp. 30-31 ff.

"Palestine" *Leviathan*, Vol. 2, No. 4 (1970), pp. 1-11.

"Palestinian People's Armed Struggle and New Awakening of the Arab People," *Peking Review*, No. 45 (November 7, 1969), pp. 18-20.

"Palestinian People's Armed Struggle Forges Ahead Victoriously," *Peking Review*, Vol. 13, No. 3 (January 16, 1970), pp. 25-28.

"Palestinian Resistance Neutralized, but not Eliminated," *Middle East Information Series*, Vol. 16 (November 1971), pp. 18-19.

Peretz, Don. "Arab Palestine! Phoenix or Phantom?" *Foreign Affairs*, Vol. 48, No. 2 (January 1970), pp. 322-33.

Peritz, R. "The Middle East and Southeast Asia: Linkages and Interactions," *Middle East Information Series*, No. 22 (February 1973), pp. 30-39.

Pfaff, R. "The American Military Presence in the Middle East," *Middle East Forum*, Vol. 48, No. 2 (1972), pp. 29- 42.

Pincus, L. "No—to the Ransom Demands," *Economic Review*, Vol. 25, Nos. 7-9 (July -September, 1972), pp. 3-5.

Pino, D. del. "Lebanon: A Difficult Co- existence," *Tricontinental*, Vol. 8, No. 82 (January 1973), pp. 2-12.

"Pour de nouveaux rapports avec les Palestiniens," *Eléments*, Nos. 8-9 (1971-72), pp. 67-74.

Prlja, A. "The Crisis of the Palestinian Movement," *Review of International Affairs*, Vol. 22, No. 519 (November 20, 1971), pp. 20-22.

Rafat, Amir. "Control of Aircraft Hijacking: The Law of International Civil Aviation," *World Affairs*, Vol. 134, No. 2 (Fall 1971), pp. 143-56.

"Resistance Operations during August 1971," *Arab Palestinian Resistance*, Vol. 3, No. 9 (September 1971), pp. 54-58.

Reuveny, Y. "On the Concept of Freedom of Manoeuvre," *International Problems*, Vol. 11, Nos. 3-4 (December 1972), pp. 25-28.

"Riding Shotgun," *The Economist*, Vol. 250, No. 6803 (January 12, 1974), p. 16.

Robinson, J.A. "Crisis Decision-Making: An Inventory and Appraisal of Concepts, Theories, Hypotheses and Techniques of Analysis," *Political Science Annual*, Vol. 2 (1969-70), pp. 111-48.

Rocheron, P. "Un Japonais bien tranquille," *Jeune Afrique*, No. 603 (July 29, 1972), pp. 12-16.

Rondot, P. "Deux semaines de crise en Jordanie," *Revue de Défense National*, Vol. 26 (April 1970), pp. 586-97.

———. "L'arabisme 'militant' et les deux Allemagnes," *Revue de Défense National*, Vol. 25 (December 1969), pp. 1986-93.

_____. "Le conflit de Palestine," *Revue Militaire Générale*, December 1968, pp. 602-20.

_____. "Les crises du printemps 1970 au Liban," *Revue de Défense National*, Vol. 26 (July 1970), pp. 1120-30.

_____. "Nouvelle crise en Jordanie et conjoncteur arabe (Juin 1970)," *Revue de Défense National*, Vol. 26 (August-September 1970), pp. 1288-98.

Rothstein, R. "The expanding war on terrorism," *American Zionist*, Vol. 63, No. 4 (December 1972), pp. 9-12.

Rouleau, E. "Yasser Arafat's self-criticism," *New Outlook*, 13, No. 9 (December 1970), pp. 8-11.

Ruzic, D. "La Lutte contre le terrorisme," *Le Monde Diplomatique*, No. 224 (November 1972), p. 4.

Said, E. "A Palestinian voice," *Columbia Forum*, Vol. 12 (Winter 1969), pp. 24-31.

_____. "The American Left and the Palestine issue" (in Arabic), *Shu'un Filastiniya* (Beirut), No. 7 (1972), pp. 208-12.

Sarhan, A. "The Swiss Attitude toward the Arab-Israeli Conflict in the Light of the Sentencing of the Palestinian Fedayin" (in Arabic), *Revue Egyptienne de Droit International*, Vol. 25 (1970), pp. 215-24.

Sarraj al-Din, I. "Towards a Comprehensive Plan for Arab Action" (in Arabic), *Dirasat 'Arabiya*, Vol. 5, No. 2 (1968), pp. 5-23.

Schiff, Z. "War on Terrorism," *The American Zionist*, Vol. 63, No. 3 (November 1973), pp. 14-16.

Schleifer, A. "The Emergence of Fatah," *Arab World*, 15, No. 5 (May 1969), pp. 16-20.

Schurmann, F. "On Revolutionary Conflict," *Journal of International Affairs*, Vol. 23, No. 1 (1969), pp. 36-53.

Schwadran, B. "The Soviet Role in the Middle East Crisis," *Current History*, Vol. 60, No. 353 (January 1971), pp. 13-18 ff.

Schwartz, B. "Israel Ménage le Liban" (Israel Manages Lebanon), *Jeune Afrique* (Paris), No. 481 (March 24, 1970), pp. 44-46.

"Secrets of the Armed Struggle in a Frank Discussion with the Leaders of Fatah," (in Arabic) *Al-Ahram* (Cairo), January 3, 1970.

Sha'ath, Nabil. "The Palestinian Revolution and the Peace Settlement" (in Arabic), *Shu'un Filastiniya* (Beirut), No. 23 (July 1973), pp. 4-11.

Sharabi, H. "Liberation or Settlement," *Journal of Palestine Studies*, Vol. 2, No. 2 (1973), pp. 33-48.

_____. "Next Phase for Palestinian Guerrillas: People's War," *Mid East*, Vol. 10, No. 3 (June 1970), pp. 15-17.

_____. "Palestine Resistance: Crisis and Reassessment," *Middle East Newsletter*, Vol. 5, No. 1 (January 1971), pp. 11-14.

_____. "Palestinian Radicals and Political Settlement," *Middle East Newsletter*, Vol. 5, No. 5 (August-September 1971), pp. 13-14.

_____. "The Liberation of Palestine and World Liberation" (in Arabic), *Shu'un Filastiniya* (Beirut), Vol. 1, No. 3 (1971), pp. 113-17.

Sheehan, E. "In the Flaming Streets of Amman," *New York Times Magazine*, September 27, 1970, pp. 26-27 ff.

Shehadeh, Musa. "Israel and the External Operations of the Resistance" (in Arabic), *Shu'un Filastiniya* (Beirut), No. 18 (February 1973), pp. 40-57.

Shukri, Gh. "America's Trojan Horse, or the Theory of the Attack from Within" (in Arabic), *al-Tali'ah*, No. 9 (September 1972), pp. 69-77.

"Since Jordan: The Palestinian Fedayeen," *Conflict Studies*, No. 38 (September 1973), pp. 1-18.

Sobel, J. "Terrorism—A Bitter Mistake," *Mapam Bulletin*, No. 26 (April 1973), pp. 19-21.

Stork, Joe. "The American New Left and Palestine," *Journal of Palestine Studies*, Vol. 2, No. 1 (Autumn 1972), pp. 64-69.

Suleiman, M. "Attitudes of the Arab Elite Toward Palestine and Israel," *American Political Science Review*, Vol. 67, No. 2 (July 1972), pp. 482-89.

Tackney, C. "Dealing Arms in the Middle East," *MERIP Reports*, No. 8 (March-April 1972), pp. 3-14.

"Terrorism: The Lessons of Munich," *Israel Horizons*, Vol. 20, No. 9 (September-October, 1972), pp. 11-15.

"Terrorists: Unpunished," *Economist*, Vol. 250, No. 6806 (February 2, 1974), p. 37.

"The Arab-Israeli Conflict," *Trans-Action* (special issue), Vol. 7, Nos. 9-10 (July-August 1970).

"The Cairo Accord Revealed by the Newspapers" (in French), *L'Orient* (Beirut), April 21, 1970, p. 3.

"The Finger Is Still on the Trigger," *Free Palestine* (London), Vol. 3, No. 5 (November 1970), pp. 4-5.

"The Hundred Years' War," *The Economist*, Vol. 233, No. 6584 (November 1, 1969), p. 14.

"The Middle East Crisis," *Current*, No. 121 (September 1970), pp. 52-64, with articles by E. Crankshaw, R. Keatley, M. Lerner, and the A.F.S.C.

"The Palestine Problem in Its Various Dimensions," *Middle East Forum*,

Vol. 46, No. 1 (1970), pp. 27-62. Articles by Constantine Zurayk, Burhan Dajjani, George Dib, and George Corm.

"The Palestinian Resistance Movement and the Arab-Israeli Conflict in Arabic Periodicals," *Journal of Palestine Studies*, Vol. 1, No. 2 (1972), pp. 120-32.

"The Palestinian Revolution in Its Fifth Year" (in Arabic), *Dirasat 'Arabiya*, Vol. 5, No. 3 (January-February 1969), pp. 2-5.

"The Permanent War: Arabs vs. Israelis," *Transaction*, Vol. 7, Nos. 9-10 (1970), Articles by R. Rosenzweig, G. Tamarin, D. Peretz, F. Khouri, Y. Harkabi, A. Perlmutter, and S. Avineri.

"The World, Their Battlefield," *Economist*, Vol. 234, No. 6601 (February 28, 1970), pp. 10-11.

"They Are Among Us," *Economist*, Vol. 244, No. 6733 (9 September 1972), pp. 13-14.

Thomas, Eduard. "Lebanon: Falling off the Tightrope," *Atlas*, Vol. 19, No. 4 (April 1970), pp. 44-45.

"Towards the Democratic Palestine," *Fatah*, Vol. 11, No. 2 (January 19, 1970), pp. 10-11.

"Une Interview de Abou Ammar sur les Problèmes de la Révolution," *Fath Informations*, No. 3 (February 8, 1972), pp. 15-19.

"United States Calls for Firm International Stand Against Terrorist Extortion and Blackmail," *Department of State Bulletin*, Vol. 68, No. 1761 (March 26, 1973), pp. 353-55.

"We Are in the Midst of a National Liberation Revolution and not a Social Revolution," *Fatah*, (Arab Version), January 26, 1970, p. 5.

"What Future for the Palestine Arabs?," *War/Peace Report*, Vol. 10, No. 6 (June-July 1970), pp. 3-11.

Wilkenfeld, J., et al. "Conflict Interactions in the Middle East," *Journal of Conflict Resolution*, Vol. 16, No. 2 (June 1972), pp. 135-54.

Winston, H. "Black Americans and the Middle East Conflict," *Political Affairs*, Vol. 49, No. 9 (September 1970), pp. 4-15.

Wolf, J. "Lebanon: The Politics of Survival," *Current History*, Vol. 62, No. 365 (January 1972), pp. 20-24.

_____. "Responses to Terrorism: Self-defense or Reprisal?," *International Problems*, Vol. 12, Nos. 1-2 (July 1973), pp. 28-33.

_____. "Shadow Over Lebanon," *Current History*, Vol. 38, No. 341 (January 1970), pp. 21-26.

_____. "The Palestinian Resistance Movement," *Current History*, Vol. 60, No. 353 (January 1971), pp. 26-31 ff.

Yaari, Ehud. "Al-Fath's Political Thinking," *New Outlook* (Tel Aviv), Vol. 2, No. 9 (November-December 1968), pp. 20-32.

———. "Fedayeen at the Crossroads: Moment of Truth for Arafat," *New Middle East*, No. 57 (June 1973), pp. 4-6.

———. "The Decline of al-Fatah," *Midstream*, Vol. 17, No. 5 (May 1971), pp. 3-12.

Yafe, R. "The UN and the Terrorist Menace," *Israel Horizons*, Vol. 20, No. 9 (September-October 1972), pp. 9-10, 21.

Yalin-Mar, N. "A Letter to a Black September Fighter," *Middle East International*, No. 22 (April 1973), pp. 14-16.

Yasin, 'Abdal-Qadr. "The Palestinian Annual Revolution" (in Arabic), *Al-Katib*, No. 146 (May 1973), pp. 103-9.

Yazid, Mohammed. "Algeria and the Arab-Israeli Conflict, an Interview," *Journal of Palestine Studies*, Vol. 1, No. 2 (Winter 1972), pp. 3-18.

Yodfat, Aryeh. "The Soviet Version and the Palestine Guerrillas," *Mizan*, Vol. 1, No. 1 (January-February 1969), pp. 8-17.

Young, Lewis. "American Blacks and the Arab-Israeli Conflict," *Journal of Palestine Studies*, Vol. 2, No. 1 (Autumn 1972), pp. 70-85.

Yusuf, A., et al. "The Arab National Liberation Movement after October 6: Problems and Horizons" (in Arabic), *al-Tali'ah*, Vol. 10, No. 1 (January 1974), pp. 10-40.

Index

Index

Abdullah ibn Hussein (King of Jordan), 44, 45, 47
Abu Ali Iyad, 84
al-Ansar, 29
  ideology, 38-39
al-Banna, Sabri, 96
al-Budayri, Misbah, 21
al-Futuwah, 8
Algeria, 43, 100
al-Husayni, Haj Muhammad Amin (Mufti), 4, 6, 7, 9, 13, 45, 48, 91, 92
al-Kayid, Abu Yusif, 16-17
al-Nabulsi, Sulayman, 47-48
al-Qaddumi, Faruq, 20
al-Sadat, Anwar, 14, 74, 95, 99
al-Sartawi, Isam, 28, 74
an-Najjadah, 8
Arab Communist parties, 38-39, 47
Arab Executive Committee, 4, 6
Arab League, 8, 10, 11, 12, 42, 93
Arab Liberation Army, 8
Arab Liberation Front (ALF), 15, 21, 22, 24, 28, 95
  ideology, 36-38, 42
Arab Nationalist Movement, 12-13
Arab Nationalist Youth Organization, 84
Arab Organization for the Liberation of Palestine (AOLP), 28, 73-74
Arafat, Yasser, 12, 15, 16, 17-18, 21, 22, 23, 24, 25, 28, 30, 34, 38, 55, 69, 72, 73, 89, 98, 99
ash-Shuqairy, Ahmad, 11, 12, 13, 48, 93, 94, 96, 98
Assad, Hafez, 95, 99
as-Sa'iqa, 14, 15, 19, 27, 28, 70, 72, 95
  ideology, 36-38

Ba'th Party, 36, 37, 47
Black September Organization (BSO), 16, 17, 57, 84-85, 86, 88
British Mandate, 1, 5, 32, 91, 92

British White Paper (1939), 8
Bustani, Emile (General), 61n, 69

Cairo Accord (1969), 15, 34n, 67-69, 71

Egypt, 9, 10, 21, 34, 42, 48, 63, 76, 92, 93, 96, 100

Fatah, 12, 13, 15, 16, 17, 19, 20, 24, 25-26, 28, 42, 43, 50, 51, 52, 56-57, 63, 66, 67, 70, 73, 84, 85, 88, 89, 90, 94, 95, 96, 97, 98, 99
  ideology, 30-32, 34-35, 37-38, 43
Fedayeen, 9, 10, 42, 92
Franjieh, Suleiman, 73

Gaza Strip, 9, 10, 11, 12, 41, 42, 92, 100, 101
Gemayel, Pierre, 73
Geneva Conference, 23, 99
Ghaffur, Ahmad, 95
guerrilla operations, 17, 52-57, 60-75

Habash, George, 12, 15, 22, 26
Hammudah, Yahya, 13
Hawatmeh, Nayif, 12, 23, 26, 27, 30, 88
Helou, Charles, 63, 64
Herzl, Theodore, 1
Higher Arab Committee, 6, 7, 90
Histadrut, 5
Hussein ibn Talal (King of Jordan), 10, 23, 45, 47, 48, 50, 52, 55, 99

Intra Bank, 62
Iraq, 10, 11, 14, 21, 26, 37, 38, 42, 95, 96, 98, 100
Israel, 9, 10, 13, 17, 35, 36, 37, 41, 42, 59, 61, 63, 64, 65, 66, 67, 71, 72, 75, 77, 85, 86, 87, 88, 89, 90, 92, 93, 97, 98, 100
Istiqlal Party, 4, 8

Jabril, Ahmad, 24, 27

137

About the Authors

Paul A. Jureidini, Vice President of Abbott Associates, Inc., of Alexandria, Virginia, is an internationally respected Middle East specialist. He was born in Lebanon and has travelled frequently and extensively throughout the Middle East. He has been involved in numerous Middle East studies for the United States government, and has served actively as a consultant to educational, commercial, financial, and law organizations, as well as government institutions. His consulting and lecturing have focused particularly on the Levant. Dr. Jureidini received the M.A. from the University of Virginia and the Ph.D. from the American University in Washington, D.C.

William E. Hazen, a Middle East specialist, has prepared a great number of studies on diverse aspects of the Middle East. In recent years, he has devoted considerable time to the Palestinian movement—its internal dynamics and its impact on and relations with regional governments and societies. Dr. Hazen, a research analyst with Abbott Associates, Inc., travels often to the Middle East, particularly Lebanon, and has written extensively on minority religious and ethnic communities and on subcultures in the Middle East. He received the M.A. from the American University of Beirut, and the Ph.D. from the Johns Hopkins University's School of Advanced International Studies in Washington, D.C.